Befriending Betsy

Befriending Betsy

A Memoir

Betsy Pauly
and Jen Braaksma

SWP
SHE WRITES PRESS

Published in 2025 by
She Writes Press, an imprint of The Stable Book Group

32 Court Street, Suite 2109
Brooklyn, NY 11201
https://shewritespress.com

Library of Congress Control Number: 2025911611

ISBN: 979-8-89636-020-9
eISBN: 979-8-89636-020-9

Interior Designer: Andrea Reider

Printed in the United States
Names and identifying characteristics have been changed to protect the privacy of certain individuals.

To all the kind souls who help stray and abandoned animals,
especially when it's not convenient for them to do so.

Introduction

On Betsy Pauly's gravestone is an inscription: "Sure Had Fun." And another: "Spay Your Pets."

I haven't seen it myself, at least not in person, though Betsy's husband, Chips, sent me photos. But the minute I saw the pictures, I immediately knew how *Betsy* the engravings were.

Yet I've never met her. I can never meet her. She died five years before I even knew she'd been alive. In an alternate world where she had lived, I suspect we never would have crossed paths. She was American; I'm Canadian. She was fifty-eight when she died; that would have made me forty-four. She was a visual artist; I cannot draw stick figures to save my life. But she was also a writer, and *now* we had something in common. Writing, then, is what drew us together.

Writing, then, bridged the gap between life and death. Decades ago, when I was in journalism school, I read an old profile of Ernest Hemingway. The reporter had accompanied the literary icon as he went shopping for a coat. I was fascinated "watching" this famous author carry out something as ordinary and mundane as buying clothes—and even more so intrigued at the experience of the reporter who got to accompany him. Hemingway came to life on the page in a fundamentally different way than the life he breathed into his stories. If I hadn't been before, I most certainly was then, a believer in the power of a narrative to help us understand others. Biographies, memoirs, anecdotes, interviews, they were all media privileging us with glimpses of the inner lives of those we could otherwise never know.

But many of those stories that I admired over the years hinged on one of two things: *another* person let us into the subject's world, like the journalist who followed Hemingway on his errands, or the subject themselves crafted their stories in ways they controlled.

With Betsy, I could do neither. I could not interview her; no coat shopping for the two of us, and while she had a draft of a manuscript, it wasn't a memoir. She had stories to tell, but they weren't specifically designed by her to purposely reveal her true self. She was an animal-welfare advocate, and she believed strongly in caring for creatures who could not care for themselves. She had a ton of crazy, wild, silly, heartbreaking, heartwarming animal stories and wanted to jot them down—but even the stories themselves weren't originally her idea.

Mother told me to write a book about my cats, Betsy writes in the introduction to her first draft. *After my allergic reaction to such advice wore off, I had to admit it was a pretty good idea, seeing as I presided over a pet-heavy household. I'd always had a hankering to write the right idea, some earthshaking tale to tell, and I recalled the familiar landscapes of my feline-filled world. Goldilocks and the Thirteen Sofa Shredders. Snow White keeps collecting really*

hairy dwarves. I had a crazy quilt of patchwork pussycat stories.

Betsy's focus was on the cats she owned, the cats she adopted, the cats she fostered, and a good number of dogs, too. She was clear to address her intended readers: cat people. She warns away the rest. ***The charm of these flighty anarchists might fall a paw short for you unfortunate folks who've never savored the highly addictive taste for Tabby, either by innocent omission or purposeful avoidance.***

As such, Betsy's intent with her writing was never to navel-gaze. She had not ventured into her project with the express idea to "tell her story." She wanted to tell her cats' stories. And dogs'. There's also a cantankerous goose, blind one-footed pigeons, and raccoons who make cameos, but Betsy's main event was cats, cats, cats. Not herself.

Yet scholars and authors dig for understanding of the deceased all the time. They read old letters, papers, manuscript drafts, and other treasures in passionate efforts to unearth their subjects and bring them back to life. Shakespeare, for example, cannot be interviewed, yet one can drown in the vast quantities of pages written about him in the last four hundred–plus years. Even Sappho, the famous Greek lyric poetess, has contemporary scholars scouring her writing 2,500 years later—and with only 650 lines of her estimated ten thousand lines of poetry remaining.

So why, then, was I surprised when I read Betsy's draft of her animal stories? Chips had found me because he wanted help getting Betsy's writing out into the world as an honor to his late wife. I'd reworked plenty of manuscripts in the past—part of my job as a book coach, editor, and ghostwriter, though I admit that until now, I'd always had access to the writer themselves. Still, it was not new to discover that a writer's prose could reveal the writer herself to her reader. Yet I could not understand why I couldn't shake ***Betsy***—not just her cats—from my head. What was it about her draft, her work, her stories that made me feel not just that I was reading about her experiences, not just that I was reading about ***her***, but that I was ***meeting*** her? How had she made me feel, simply by reading her work, that I was ***already*** her friend?

I had to find out.

Chapter 1

My first clue was laughter. Gut-punching, glorious, slapstick laughter. My first thought: Oh my God, I want to meet this woman who stripped out of her pantyhose one afternoon in downtown Dallas to rein in a meandering mutt! Not simply *This story is hilarious, I can just picture it!* But specifically, I wanted to meet Betsy. I wanted to ask her about the experience she'd put on paper; I wanted to explore the details of that day.

Immediately I was reminded of a favorite quote from J. D. Salinger's *The Catcher in the Rye*. Holden Caulfield is a frustrated, mentally distressed teen who wanders New York because he feels like he can't go home. He's lonely and isolated, and he craves connection, something he searches for throughout the story. He talks about his love of books: "What really knocks me out is a book that, when you're all done reading it, you wish the author that wrote it was a terrific friend of yours and you could call him up on the phone whenever you felt like it."

That's how I felt after reading "The Discombobulated Dog." Only, maybe I took it one step further. Maybe I already did think of Betsy as a friend, and maybe for a split second,

I did want to contact her—until my rational brain kicked in. Obviously I couldn't contact her.

Obviously I'd never even have the chance to meet her.

The sharp pang of sadness surprised me. It was lightning quick, there and gone, but real nonetheless. I was sad that I'd never get to talk with her, see her animated face over a video call (because I was assuming her face would have been animated, based on the gregarious tone of her stories).

I've experienced grief before; my dad, with whom I was very close, died when I was in my twenties. I've lost my grandparents. I've lost friends. And students. When I was a high school teacher, some of my hardest days were when I had to step into class and face an empty seat. There's a spectrum, a continuum of grief, where some losses affect you more than others, the hurt deeper or less severe, depending. I didn't know Betsy, I'd never met Betsy, yet, as I read about her adventures with a "pony-sized wild dog" in the heart of a city I'd never been to, I felt a familiar ache. Sadness.

But then I kept reading. And Betsy kept me laughing. She was a woman of determination, that's for sure. By the end of the story, the sadness had morphed into a smile. Wow, I wish I had met her.

The Discombobulated Dog

My husband Chips and I would end up, for some of our years together, in our own little Mayberry—Carthage, Missouri, our tiny see-all/tell-all society. It was so different, coming from our Dallas days of minding our blissfully anonymous business.

Or was it?

As I sat down to set down my tomcat tomfoolery, I initially thought I'd be writing about our new impromptu bed-and-breakfast venture—for the four-legged variety of guests—in our new hometown, but my thoughts drifted to Dallas.

Perhaps we—*I*—hadn't been as anonymous as I thought. On the surface, I thought that namelessly navigating a sea of self-involved human discourse in a big city suited our shy Norwegian ways, most particularly Mr. Wonderful's penchant for privacy. In my memory, he had compartmentalized his life and any crossover was strictly monitored. Case in point: Early on after my arrival from Minnesota, from which we both hailed and where we had met, several lady callers were shocked—and understandably dismayed—to hear long after the fact that their number one go-to bachelor had gone and tied the knot. Chips's matrimonial life, it seemed, had been tightly sealed from other parts of it. He kept his lips as hermetically sealed in his work as a lawyer, too, ensuring his major-league clients did not drown in any dicey drama. Poker-face Pauly had a built-in gag order, the gold standard of lawyerly loyalty.

Imagine, then, that stoic pillar of jurisprudence nestled in his office sixty stories above the bustle of the city, getting an earful, at work, of his wife's shenanigans.

Cass, his brother-in-law, gleefully got to his point: "Your wife was being dragged along the sidewalk behind a pony-sized wild dog, harnessed, it seems, by Mrs. Pauly's pantyhose."

No doubt my utterly unflappable sweetheart handled the bizarre recounting with good humor, but I suspect *he* never suspected his work-here/play-there worlds could collide in such a freaky fashion.

So much for anonymity.

I'd been downtown that day when I'd spotted a sorry skeleton of a tail-wagger, an unquestionably underfed dog living in an unforgiving asphalt jungle, alone and adrift among the churning currents of oblivious people. And in desperate need of a friend.

I was on the job.

I did my due diligence. I asked around about the mutt, but my plethora of earnest "pardon me, sir" utterances garnered only suspicious side sneers. We were alone. I looked at him. He looked at me.

"Yes, you're coming with me," I told him.

Only . . . *how?*

We were several blocks from the parking garage and my car; he was not my well-trained pet who would easily follow. But he *was* waist-high and much too cumbersome to cradle. Oh, and he was a very artful—and supersonic—darter at that. I didn't dare leave him to his own two-minute mile in the tangle of the noon-hour hubbub to search out some kind of tether. I had no belt—my dressed-up-for-downtown duds did not assume a makeshift dog leash would be necessary—and my one-handed rummaging through my bottomless handbag did not turn up anything remotely rope-ish. Mary Poppins, I was not. But as I dodged the hyper dog's legs, my own came to mind. Well, not my legs, per say, but rather my now-torn stockings on my legs. Perhaps my dressed-up-for-downtown duds *did* assume a makeshift dog leash after all. So, amid a swarm of bumper-to-bumper passersby in downtown Dallas in the middle of a workday, I stripped out said stockings and tied them securely around my new furry, attention-deficit friend.

And you know what? The pantyhose became the perfect restraint for my new raging beast. Every dog has his day of learning who's in charge, and this bucking bronco had a steep learning curve. Perhaps, if you are a dog lover, you may remember *your* maiden voyage behind a clueless, rocket-propelled pooch. Perhaps you remember the chaos. Now, if you had a pip-squeak cockapoo, it would have been no problem, right? But picture that same fish-on-the-line fight from a fifty-pound hound dog. With bungee-cord tension from a pantyhose leash. I may have shrieked, un-alpha-like, as we slalomed through the human obstacle course.

But it worked! My MacGyvering got us both to the car, though I felt as if I'd hauled in the catch of the day instead of a down-on-his-luck dog.

Only, driving turned out not to be much easier, with an eager pooch's paws-on attempts to take the wheel. Miraculously, I missed all the unsuspecting fellow motorists.

And then! Then! My discombobulated dog, so intent on disrupting the car ride, wouldn't budge from his shotgun position when we arrived home. As if I had power-lift potential to heave him out!

Alas, I had no choice, and heave-ho I did, into the happy-pack house and I laid out the rules. Show-me-some-class-use-the-grass hygiene; let's keep snoopy snouts out of no-nose zipper zones; all four on the floor (all tall orders for my touchy-feely Fred Astaire).

I hadn't truly thought of how to explain this beast in our bathtub to my Mr. Play-It-Cool Pauly when he arrived home—and had no plans to explain the "hows" of my day. I'd been counting on the statistical certainty of hauling a barking, heifer-sized dog incognito and therefore keeping the details well under my Crazy Stray Lady hat. After all, if Chips could compartmentalize his life, then so, too, could I.

It was not that I had any intention of lying, but a sage piece of fatherly advice floated back to me. "Betsy," my dad had told me upon my nuptials, "the happiest of marriages don't always adhere to an unwavering spill-all-the-beans policy." No doubt, he was anticipating his little girl's big mouth might rock her newly launched Love Boat just a wee bit. (No doubt he might have had cause for concern.) Of course, since I was floating high on a honeymoon cloud, I had immediately pooh-poohed his words of wisdom as cynical censorship. What did he know, a man married for decades? But time and a few pillow-talk bumps and bruises brought me around to Dad's way of thinking. Turns out some things *are* better left unsaid between Mr. and Mrs. Surely a midday downtown striptease counted in that category. What would be the benefit of bemoaning my hairy rush-hour roundup? My beloved was congenitally wired to worry; no need to add fuel to his protective fire.

Yet in he walked that evening, with the whole instant replay on his tongue.

So much for anonymity.

But instead of worry, for which there was no need, given that both the beast of a dog and I had survived, Chips declared instead that the outlandish (and nearly indecent) incident was highly amusing. An urban legend of our lives.

Ah, but I had the last laugh when Chips's hee-hawing simmered down to a sad-clown grimace. He was staring at the beast in the bathtub, eagerly awaiting his bubbly baptism like he was set for his first teacup ride at the fair, but all idle excitement ended when the faucet's flow transformed that once-calm Pig-Pen into a cyclonic soaking mop of furry fury. Turns out *we* were in for a tilt-a-whirl of a ride. It was wash-and-rinse mayhem as we tried to clean the hydrophobic dog, but we were well rewarded, finally, with rapid-fire kisses from our squeaky-clean mountain of fluff.

He wouldn't be staying, of course. We weren't his forever home, so I searched for someone who could be. I found Mrs. Perfect.

And though I talked up how smart and wonderful he was—a picture of canine congeniality and comportment, a first-class Family Guy, with a don't-worry-be-happy tail wag—I did have to warn her. "It's guaranteed, there'll be mad dashes out the door."

Over a tall glass of reserve chardonnay in her dazzling parlor, Mrs. Perfect placidly assured me of her commitment to contain her new high-octane housemate, and, on paper, it seemed an idyllic match. She had oodles of spare time and money, even a bolt-proof Berlin Wall–ed backyard for our four-legged Ferrari.

Some few blissfully boring weeks later, I received a mystifying message from a perturbed caller, wondering if I would *please* collect my freewheeling dog and keep it confined to its *own* grass and garbage.

I glanced with great confusion at our own dog, Daisy May, a terrier who, committed couch potato that she was, had never answered the call of the running-wild. She looked up at me, innocence all over her face. *Who, me?*

The old gent must have misdialed, and I started to tell him as much—until he described a passing flash of fur flying down the block at breakneck speed, wearing our furry-411 dog tag.

Annoyed, but not with him, I stuttered out proxy apologies for such sloppy house-hound-keeping, then I rounded up and returned the happy-go-lucky roadrunner to Mrs. Perfect. She'd been oblivious to her new dog's jailbreak. She offered me a lukewarm "you-again" look and a "good-riddance" goodbye (but not a "thanks for giving Rover a ride home") and meager reassurance that she'd not only keep an eye on her furry Forrest Gump but also update his dog tag. Soon.

Not soon enough.

Weeks later, the same crabby caller read me the riot act. It seemed my not-so-social house call had done nothing to mend Mrs. (Not-So) Perfect's ways; the neighborhood streaker was again on the loose. I had to count to ten—twice—to calm myself before I schlepped over to pick up the Lone Ranger and return him to his alleged address.

"What's the big deal?" Mrs. Perfect waved me off.

Mind your own business, her hissy fit said.

I had to bite my tongue, wondering if there was anything to energize Mrs. Perfect from her indifferent state of inertia.

Strike three.

This time, it wasn't grumbling Grandpa ("Get your damn dog!") but a Good Samaritan in a decrepit public housing project many miles from the dog's hypothetical home, urging me to hurry as a gang of budding bad boys began to torment the trusting wanderer.

Worried sick—and mad as hell at the apathy of his guardian (in name only)—I plucked poor Cinder-fella from his latest peril. I was torn between hope and dread at receiving a halfhearted call from Doggy-Mommy Dearest, but nope, nada. I scoured for any signs of a *lost love of our life* poster, but double nada. I frightened myself by imagining my poor Iditarod-wannabe without our hound-hotline dog tag (his *only* get-out-of-trouble card), back on the mean streets and gone forever, succumbing to some sad, unknown furry fate. It was time to own up to a major BFF-brokering mistake.

Having sincerely requested *Sure Had Fun* to be carved upon my gravestone, right under *Don't forget to fix Fido and Fluffy!*, I suspected Chips would wearily add the all-time-broken-record Betsy-ism forever ringing in his ears: *It's all meant to be!* And yet it hadn't been meant to be, not at all. I stripped bare for this dog in downtown Dallas (okay, just my legs); I would not let him disappear. But what to do? I wallowed for a while, stinging with self-flagellation. I had messed up.

And then, like providence had tossed me a bone, the perfect people showed up.

Each summer, Chips and I welcomed Emillie and James, our half-grown niece and nephew, hoping to mentor these children of divorce in what wedded bliss looked like (as so excellently exemplified by me and Mr. Wonderful—no need to be humble about being happy). They loved coming. They had 24-7 access to our swarming stable of furry friends—a Christmas-in-July level of happiness, since four-footed friends were strictly verboten in their townhouse—and unlimited pool access for jackknifes and cannonballs just outside the back door. It was always a raucous waterlogged whirligig when they visited, especially when Uncle Chips would continuously launch the relentless minnows into tidal waves of fun.

It was not surprising, then, that one of my turned-up tabbies, a recent rescue, would claim space in my niece's heart. That left poor James without a fur-buddy of his own. As it happened, James's mother was lamenting her lonely boy's growing pains, just as I was saving our dog-sprinter for the last hair-raising time.

A conversation or two later, *et voilà*! Within a week, a crate of guaranteed good, clean fun arrived in baggage claim full of the soon-to-be Scooter. (New gig, new name.) This new BFF fit like a (fifty-nine-pound) glove into the now-pet-friendly family. He was finally running (sprinting, tearing) with the right crowd. No surprise, the incorrigible escape artist still bolted at every tempting crack of the door, but those Kentucky Derby dashes were just fifty-yard flashes with his hotfooted housemates fast on those four heels.

In the end, when it comes right down to the bare (doggy) bones necessities, our barking buddies' needs are pretty simple: a high-and-dry den, plenty of chow, a good stretch of the legs, and someone to slobber all over.

In spite of a change in status from Mrs. Perfect's chardonnay-filled lifestyle to a hand-me-down, Hamburger Helper budget, Scooter thrived in his new home. (Despite his hasty snack choice of a brand-new bedspread.) And though he never did charm his fellow freeloader, the cat, into any kind of weekday fun, he nevertheless gleefully installed himself at the center of his split-level-ranch universe. He would strategically station himself under the linoleum breakfast table for maximum morning saliva-tations to every adored ankle, then later plop himself on his sofa-top sinkhole, snout glued to well-smeared window, waiting for his people, and then run off—*with* his people—down Lucky Dog Lane.

And all because it was obvious for everyone to see that day in downtown Dallas—including my husband's coworkers—that I would do whatever I could, including stripping off my own clothes, to save a stray.

Anonymous, indeed.

When I was thirteen, my parents had an addition built on our house. Only the foundation had been poured when a mangy mutt appeared on the concrete ledge early one fall morning. We'd lived in the neighborhood all my life; we knew our neighbors' dogs, and this wasn't one of them. The air was cold and crisp, so my mom, reluctantly, brought the pup into the house. He had no tag, though he looked relatively well-fed. Mom started to call around to see if anyone knew or recognized the mystery dog, to no avail.

My thirteen-year-old self got super excited.

"Can we keep him, ***pleeeease?***" We had no dogs, no cats, no rabbits, hamsters, gerbils, guinea pigs, rabbits, birds, or even fish. We were a pet-free home. I had been trying to rectify that for years. Providence smiled upon me in the form of a stray dog.

Mom glowered at me, though I'm sure she was also suppressing a laugh. "You know we can't. Your sister is allergic."

"So?" I truly failed to see the problem. She was taking allergy shots, she'd be fine. Maybe.

"A dog isn't good for her."

"So?"

Mom sighed. "It's either the dog or your sister."

Oh my god! A solution! "Well, the ***dog***, of course!"

For reasons I failed to understand, my mom chose my sister. She swept me out of the house, even as I clung, for one last hug, to the well-mannered pooch, and off to school. When I returned home, the dog was gone. (But the sister was still there.)

Mom hadn't found the owners; she'd taken him to the local pet shelter. I never found out what happened to him.

"I named him Addition," I told my family that night.

"You named a dog that was here for all of an hour and that you'll never see again?" my sister asked, incredulous.

Given that she was responsible for me never seeing the dog again, I huffed. "Yes."

I had done nothing to search out that stray; I had done nothing to care for him (unless a million hugs counted). He appeared literally in my backyard and disappeared as quickly, but in my mind, he was ***mine***.

As the years passed—in the same pet-free household, alas—my love for animals dissipated. I'd given up on persuading my parents (***still***, they insisted on keeping my sister), and "borrowing" my best friend's husky wasn't the same.

Then along came a visit to a friend's farm. I'd met my future husband by that point, and, as we toured the barns, two tiny orange fluffballs followed us everywhere.

"They're barn cats," our friend explained. "We don't feed them or take care of them."

I was aghast. How could no one care for these cute-as-a-button creatures?

"You can take them, if you want." Our friend waved at the kittens offhandedly.

And just like that, Scott and I had two new additions.

I hadn't thought about that dog, or the origins of our first pair of cats, for a long time, until I read Betsy's story. The dog had simply appeared, and the cats, big personalities that they were, insisted on making their presence known. I'd had to do no work to "rescue" the animals, so I was enthralled by the humorous lengths to which Betsy would go for a poor stray.

"Who *does* that?" I muttered to myself, laughing, still picturing Betsy peeling off her pantyhose, one-handed, to leash the hulking speedster of a dog.

Not only was my curiosity piqued; so, too, was my admiration. Here was a woman unafraid to do what she felt was right. How many other people had walked by the dog, unseeing? Or unassuming? How many others had steered clear of the boisterous beast? No doubt, I would have been one of them, but Betsy wasn't.

Yet it wasn't just her boldness that caught my attention, nor her bubbly tone with which she recounted her tale. It was that the story started with mention of her husband. She was, from the first, aware of herself through an outsider's view. Was she truly worried what Chips would think? Not in the least, as Chips himself would confirm when we spoke. Yet still, she could appreciate her antics from a different perspective. And she didn't take herself too seriously. The welfare of her rescues, most definitely she took seriously; the first draft of her descriptions of Mrs. Perfect were . . . vitriolic . . . but of her own role, she kept it light.

"She had terrific sense of humor," Chips told me. "She enjoyed laughing a lot, she enjoyed people who were fun, and she didn't enjoy people who were not fun."

Confirmation.

And from one story alone.

But it was also Betsy's very own comments about her gravestone that choked me up. Chips had explained, as he shared a picture of it, that Betsy had insisted on the inscription. Her choice was unconventional, to say the least, and Chips could have reneged on his promise. But he hadn't, and he didn't, because she had "sincerely requested ***Sure Had Fun*** to be carved upon my gravestone, right under ***Don't forget to fix Fido and Fluffy!***" (Okay, so Chips paraphrased . . .)

She had *sincerely* requested the unconventional. Here were her wishes, in black and white, written before her death. It wasn't just Chips's interpretation of her wishes; she'd made herself clear.

This is who I am, this one story cried out.

And one word echoed in my head:

Authentic.

Chapter 2

Imaginative, too.

Betsy came to me on the page. Her words were all she had, yet vividly, she painted pictures worthy of her own visual art.

Her language wasn't perfect; it was a draft, after all, from which I was working. In one tale of two dogs, she wrote, "After a three-second back scratch, my foot-long-hothead went belly up, Mr. Bring-it-ON! suddenly silly putty in my hands, enraptured in a tummy tickle-induced trance. His careworn alter ego soaked up all that heavenly Happy-Pack hugging and kissing but absolutely refused to enter Big Beta's den, unbudgeable as Buddha, utterly unmoved by beef bribery, lowly begging and every last ounce of pushing and pulling I had in me (his hoagie-sized pal blindly tailed Sugar Mama wheresoever I and my Milk-Bones wandered.)"

It took me a minute to parse through her figurative language, but that in and of itself spoke volumes. Most non-writers (okay, and most writers), if they think about it at all, assume that what appears on the page in front of them is what appeared, like magic, from the mind of the author. But nothing could be further from the truth. Unless one is a literary genius (and though I hear they exist, in all my years in the writing business, I have not yet met one capable of a completely clean first draft), the first (and second and fourth and twentieth) draft will look far from perfect—***as a final version***. It is, of course, perfect in its "first-draftness," because the purpose of a first draft is ***only*** to get ideas down on paper. They are ***not*** to have every theme, character, plot point, and nuance brilliantly conveyed all at once. It is an impossible feat, like assuming Hollywood blockbusters were filmed, as we see them fully put together on the screen, in one take.

You see, stories are a language. They live in a perfect form in the imagination of the writer. Like your dreams, for example. But when you try to explain your dreams the next morning? "Well, it was my house, but not my house, and you were there, only it wasn't you, and you had three heads, and it was in Africa, but not really because there was snow on the beach . . ." How, then, can you convey ***precisely*** what you experienced when our language is so limiting? That's what writing is: the translation of ideas into words that other people can understand. We take what's clear to us in our imaginations, and then we work to interpret them into a language you, the reader, can understand. Words, phrases, sentences, paragraphs, chapters. All in a structure you come to expect and anticipate. All in a way that makes sense. ***In a two-story house with a vaulted ceiling, set back from the beach on Zanzibar, by the Indian Ocean, a strange, freakish snowstorm erupted, as if Mount Kilimanjaro, Africa's tallest peak, 250 miles away, were crying white fluffs of tears. It was as strange and unexpected as me imagining you with three heads.***

From imagination to words, to a ***story***.

Betsy did not have the chance to polish her words before she died, but what language she did leave us was rife with her extraordinary imagination.

Mutt & Jeff Joke

Some of us are cat people, others strictly for the dogs, but anyone lucky enough to commune among hordes of either furry flavor knows how well they, well, resemble *us*. They can have eerily familiar political liaisons and cliquish intrigues within their own social orders and disorders, full of teacher's pets and catty drama queens straight out of the Hairball High yearbook. Their own pecking order keeps things at a seething simmer most of the time (kind of like real high school), but when all household hell breaks loose, it's every freeloader for himself.

But occasionally, you can find the exact opposite, where Pup One and Pup Two are forever superglued to the pack, ingrained into their indelible cave-dog DNA that demands a backup buddy when things get dicey. We often think of pooch pals as a matched set—double-vision litter look-alikes, a pair of yippy-yappy floor dusters, a duo of hounds as big as houses—but what makes us laugh are the comically clashing K9 couples, the strangest sorts of doggy-bedfellows.

Let me tell you about one mind-boggling mismatch.

During our Dallas days, we lived a remarkably Zen life for certified city slickers. Our house was but a stone's throw from a people-lined little lake, a popular oasis for two-footed meanderers and ten-speed racers, and every kind of weekend warrior in between. There were, too, the standard beach-blanket, sun-soaking water worshippers, some of whom, I'm furious to say, deemed the crowded shoreline the perfect spare-pet repository. I don't know their thought process. Did they assume—most cruelly and irrationally—that their unwanted mutts were but inconvenient car chasers, litter makers, and time and money takers? Did they decide the dogs were as disposable as old hush puppies? Did they truly think their canines could sustain themselves alone among the not-so-natural resources? (Wrong, wrong, *wrong*; might as well drop them on the moon.) Did they assume that other park-goers would pick up lost little Lassie? As if Fido could just flag down Joe Jogger with his *will wag for treats sign* and seal the deal . . .

But they must think something because those bottom-of-the-barrel humans routinely dumped man's and woman's best friend alongside their Sunday-afternoon garbage. I know this to be true—both that they're bottom-of-the-barrel humans (because who could be so cruel?) and that they dumped their dogs—because a few sad furry castaways would fatefully find their way to our revolving doggy door.

One morning when I was blearily retrieving the *Morning News*, a flash of color caught my precaffeinated line of sight. I saw a Laurel-and-Hardy dog team fly by and I truly did have to do a double-take. There was a stubby little dachshund, an adorable overstuffed bratwurst on four feet, running alongside a German shepherd, the size of a burglar's worst nightmare. The ground-hugger ran at full throttle, frantically keeping pace with his big buddy's easy trot. I laughed at the image in my mind: the Animal Planet's answer to the irrepressible

Danny DeVito and Arnold Schwarzenegger duo in the movie *Twins*. The cartoon churn of the little one's legs and the loping lengths of the big guy spoke volumes. These were no cavorting, scent-sniffing AWOL day-trippers; instead they charged ahead in a desperate search for their missing owners (i.e., the jackasses who shoved them out of cars).

I yoo-hooed them on their second sprint around the block, but my calls only revved their manic *run* command. I knew what to do. By lap three, they slammed to a sudden stop. They sniffed the air with a wishful whiff of my recently retrieved treats. Gently, I tiptoed toward the Odd Couple. And if I didn't bust out a laugh when Junior planted himself directly *under* his towering comrade and let loose a ferociously full-sized diatribe. His bodyguard kept still. Ah, the strong, silent type. And as hard as the half-pint was trying, I really was more inclined to give Mr. Big some breathing room. Herculean heft, it seemed, spoke louder than the little guy's tough talk. I sat down and stayed still as a statue. They looked at me, wary and guarded, but hunger prevailed over hard-knocks caution, and gently our standoff dissipated. They gobbled up my treats, gorging themselves, as I crab-crawled slowly, steadily, stealthily. I would freeze at their slightest frisson, then resume my slithering as they returned to their frantic refueling. Finally, I could grab their treasured bait bowls and lure them away from the dangerous traffic.

With their stomachs sated, the drifters reappraised their Lunch Lady, now conceding to some belly rubs and soft talk. It took only a three-second back scratch for my foot-long hothead to turn belly up. Mr. Bring It *On* was suddenly Silly Putty in my hands. He was enraptured in a tummy-tickle trance. Firmly won over, he was quite content to tail his new Sugar Mama wheresoever I and my Milk-Bones wandered. His careworn colleague was another story. While he, too, soaked up all the heavenly hugging and kissing, he absolutely refused to come inside. Unbudgeable as Buddha, no amount of beef bribery, lowly begging, or even the very last ounce of pushing and pulling I had in me would move him.

I feared their post-fiesta flight as I cooked up plan B, so I foolishly tethered both Felix and Oscar to our front porch. As much as the little guy would have followed me anywhere, it felt wrong to check my little brown shadow into our hairy hostel while his big buddy remained outside. There was little doubt that my midget motormouth and his "twin" must have met up on that long road to nowhere. I just didn't have the heart to bust up their hilarious hound-stacking act.

It seemed like a good idea.

It turned out to be a seriously stupid and idiotic idea. In hindsight, I can only claim temporary crazier-than-usual-Cat-Lady insanity. I was duly punished as I now had to unweave their spiderwebs from around porch pillars, potted plants, flagpole, and each other. And even as I, the dimwitted detangler, tried to separate them, the bewildered knot-knitters kept up their mayhem around my every step.

But they were adorable! Surely it wouldn't take long to find their forever family. I was determined to keep them together. Alas, many weeks and want ads later, I was skunked, without a single Samaritan intrigued by my eight-pawed package deal. It didn't help when we got devastating news from the vet that muddled matters further. Our shepherd was riddled with heartworms and demanded a grueling Rx of arsenic and a dog year of bed rest ASAP.

Meanwhile, a *muy bonita* bunch of wiener-dog devotees went gaga over Señor Dachshund but declined with a *No, gracias,* to his *muchacho grande.*

And our picture-perfect neighbors (yes, there really is such a creature), the Fabulous Franneas, fell hard for the humongous hound but weren't inclined to take on a ready-made pack.

Two homes, but separated.

My heart broke a little.

But our neighbors, with their trio of gentle-giant sons and a mom who is that rarest of unicorns, a *nice* person with never a nasty word to say, agreed to patiently wait while I pounded the pavement for a double-dog home.

Some things are not meant to be. I finally had to admit defeat and break up my dynamic duo. Newly christened Lucky, the shepherd moved across the street to his dream team of a new family, and my little dachshund went to the Spanish-speaking family.

Yet I had been mistaken. I'd been so hell-bent on my power couple staying together that I'd forgotten the power of a loving home. In the end, both BFF mergers were bona fide happily ever afters. It was magical to witness the miraculous power of unconditional love on two pups who had nearly been a lost cause.

Lucky and his new troop of chronically happy campers migrated west. And though they'd declined our little one, fate has a way of intervening. The family ended up with a second shrimpy sidekick, fished out of the desert. No one, of course, was surprised at Mr. Big's affinity for another ankle-sized pal. I still smile, remembering one Christmas card featuring our old doggy friend and his new canine companion, barely squeezed into the same frame. They were decked out in twinkling holiday headgear, beaming at their beloved human behind the camera. In spite of a bottom-rung start and close brush with the four-pawed grim reaper, our former boarder blossomed in that love-me-tender tribe to a ripe old age.

Chips was living in Dallas and had been for many years when he met Betsy. He was thirty-four and single. His mother still lived in Minneapolis, and he still had friends there, having gone to both high school and college there. He returned for a visit.

The wife of his friend was hosting a group of women whom she worked with, so his friend suggested they go out. Later in the evening, when they came back to the house, a few women remained. Betsy was one of them. She'd been standing behind the counter in the kitchen.

"I saw her immediately and was taken," Chips told me. "I went over and started talking to her, putting on my typical bachelor approach to things, Dallas, Texas, style." He laughed. "She was very unreceptive to my overtures."

But she didn't walk away, so Chips kept talking. Still, after ten minutes and no indication he should continue, he said goodbye and left.

A few months later, his friend's wife called him. "Do you remember the woman you talked to at my house?"

Chips knew immediately who she was talking about. "Sure."

"She might be open to going on a date when you're here for Christmas."

He was back home for ten days; he and Betsy, nine years younger, saw each other every day. There was an instant connection. This was in those barely remembered pre-internet days, so when Chips returned to Dallas, they talked on the phone all the time. Betsy, with a degree in business administration from the University of Minnesota, was in business for herself with some partners. They were financially successful, but Betsy had always wanted to paint. When she came to a career crossroads, Chips pounced.

"I had a carriage house out back of my home, so I came up with the idea that we could turn it into an art studio for her. If we were going to get together, that was the time to make a move."

Betsy was all in; she moved to Dallas, set up her art studio, and, a year later, she and Chips got married.

Because Betsy had a business background, she wasn't satisfied with just creating art; she had to market it and sell it. On her own initiative, she would go to large office buildings in Dallas and make arrangements where she would set up in their lobby for two or three weeks with her artwork, and all the people coming in and out of the building would see it. She sold a lot of art to the people who worked in the buildings and to people who came through the buildings. Some of the executives even commissioned her to do work for their new offices. At the time, Betsy worked in pen and ink and oils, but she gradually shifted to work on smaller watercolor pieces, until she transitioned, yet again, to writing.

When she and Chips got together, she had a medium-sized black-and-white dog, but according to her husband, there was no precursor to her interest in animal welfare.

"We'd been camping one weekend, coming back from a lake in Oklahoma," Chips explained, "and we were on a divided highway. Betsy saw a dog in the median. 'You need to pull over. We need to pick up that dog.' That was the first time that I'd seen that side of her."

From then on, Betsy didn't bypass a stray animal. If there was a cat or dog that appeared to be on its own, she would round it up and get it rehabbed, get it socialized, and then have it adopted. She would put ads in the paper; she even had a sign put in the front yard when there were kittens or puppies available. She never sold an animal, though the adopting party would pay the spay or neuter costs, and once they moved to Carthage, Betsy set up a tax-exempt entity, the Carthage Spay Neuter Assistance Program, whose funds were used to pay the spay/neuter costs for low-income pet owners.

Betsy took her new occupation very seriously. "She'd interview the people and make sure they were responsible and financially able to adopt the animals," Chips said. " I don't know where the genesis of it was. I'd never seen or heard it before. Growing up, Betsy's family had had one cat, so it wasn't something she was exposed to all along."

But Betsy felt incredibly strongly about helping animals. She said humans domesticated them, so it was humans' responsibility to take care of them. She felt that unless somebody stepped up, the animals would suffer. They don't do well on their own, particularly dogs. Eventually, she volunteered at the humane society in Dallas.

She'd been doing volunteer work for a while; she'd worked at a women's shelter, but, as Chips explained, she found it outside her sphere of understanding. "She couldn't grasp how abused women would repeat the cycle; it made no sense to her; in her mind, once you're out, you're out, and you would never go back."

Betsy didn't deny the women had their reasons; she just felt frustrated that the cycle would repeat and she couldn't do more.

"She had a big heart," Chips said, "but she was much more sensitive to animals than humans. She didn't donate to causes; she didn't say 'Let's send money to the earthquake victims'; she didn't respond to ads on TV to send money to St. Jude's. That wasn't her nature. Kind and generous, but her focus was animals. Animal welfare. Not animal rights. She didn't say you couldn't raise pigs, but you shouldn't have the right to raise them in concentrated feeding operations. She said puppy mills should be banned. She did have a big heart, but it was not across the board. She wasn't torn by every sad situation she ever saw."

Betsy's tumble into the pet-rescue life happened slowly. She did not set out to open up a "hairy hostel," as she called their home, though fostering the animals is exactly what happened. She and Chips had their own pets, a dog and a cat or two, but Betsy always tried to adopt out the animals she found. The problem was that some animals, especially cats, did not socialize well. If you have a kitten who is too skittish to come out when prospective owners come by, you aren't going to get it adopted.

"We were at our gym one night when a little black-and-white kitten came in out of the cold," Chips remembered. "The owner threw him outside, but he came back in. Betsy picked him up and took him home and that was our third cat. And then here comes a cat that no one will adopt. Then another, and another. You've got four or five animals that are part of your home that you didn't deliberately say, 'Let's get another cat.' But Betsy refused to send an unsocial cat to the humane society because she knew it would just be put down. That was not acceptable. We were the harbor of last resort for those animals."

The numbers climbed. Betsy couldn't let them go. At their peak, they had thirteen cats.

Is it cheating that I told you some stories about Betsy before allowing you to read the rest of the stories she wrote? I only learned more about Betsy's life after I'd read her draft. Should I have allowed you the same privilege? To connect with Betsy from her words alone, the way I did?

The thing is, the questions swirled the whole time I read her work. Who *was* this woman? How did she start on this path? And, most importantly, *why*? The more I read, the more I wanted to know.

But for all my lengthy conversations with Chips, I came to realize we'd rarely focused on aspects of Betsy's life outside her stories. She was more than an animal-welfare advocate. She was an artist, a wife, a friend, a daughter, an aunt. She'd lived a full life before she first spotted the dog on the median, and she would live a full (too-short) life after she and Chips moved to Florida and their animal kingdom dwindled. And yes, had I been able to sit and chat with her over coffee (or tea? What did she prefer? I didn't know), I would have loved to hear all her escapades. As it was, though, I was drawn to the stories themselves.

"Tell me more about them," I asked Chips.

Because it was through her stories that I wanted to connect.

Chapter 3

The idea that I was *connecting* to Betsy came to me gradually. I was of course intrigued. Curious. I'd often connected with stories, as most readers can attest to, and I'd often connected with authors with whom I work. But had I connected with an author in this way before?

It puzzled me. Here's why.

I'm not actually an animal person.

For all my desire to keep that stray dog when I was thirteen, I never sought out a pet on my own. Scott was the one who opened the door for our two tiny barn cats. When they grew old and died natural, old-age deaths, it was my two then-young daughters who begged and begged and begged for more cats. (Well, truth be told, they wanted kittens, the reality that they would grow up to be adult cats a pesky future issue.) My husband was a softie. The three of them wore me down. Two cats, adopted from a pet-rescue center, were now ours.

I remember Chips telling me that no one would adopt a cat if you had to use a broom to sweep them out from under the bed, but that, in fact, is almost exactly how we were first introduced to Ivy. The rescue center had a web page and a very talented web designer, who knew how to tug at the heartstrings by posting the most aw-cute pictures ever. Ivy was front and center, the most gorgeous-colored calico. I made the mistake of showing her picture to my family; we were over at the foster home the next day. There we met Ivy's sister Holly, less shy, but only barely.

"They'll warm up to you," the foster caregiver told us.

It took five years.

But we weren't done collecting animals, oh, no. Scott came across a teeny, tiny black kitten up for adoption from the humane society. This time it was his mistake of showing it to our daughters. "I want her!" my youngest, then eight, explained. And so, Shadow became "hers." Our oldest insisted on a fish.

"Really, sweetheart? We're offering you a cat and you're choosing a fish?"

"Yep." She was stubborn that way.

The appeal of the fish soon wore off (I bit my "I-told-you-so" tongue), and a month later, Angel, cat number four, came into our lives.

Oh, and don't get me started about the two guinea pigs! Can I admit, am I a terrible mother, person, and human being to say I experienced no grief at their (thankfully) early demise?

At our pet-crazy height, we had four cats, two guinea pigs, and two fish.

And I don't love animals.

I have held firm, all these years, that we will never get a dog. All I could imagine was the *work* involved. Not the love.

Am I heartless? Would Betsy, who suffered no fools, have sent me on my way, had I held out an overture of friendship?

Since I don't abandon my animals, and I give them all the love and attention of which I'm capable, I suspect not. Betsy held her vitriol for those who abandoned, abused, or neglected their pets. I may not have a heart embroidered with fur, but never would I harm an animal.

If I *had* been an animal lover, with the same intense compassion as Betsy, then I might have more easily accepted this growing connection I felt. Common interests and all. But I did not have what Chips laughingly called Betsy's "straydar."

"Whether she was driving or a passenger, she saw stuff, things I wouldn't notice. She had an ability to recognize something was amiss. She saw them when no one else did."

That was most definitely ***not*** me. We were therefore not two kindred spirits on the one topic about which Betsy writes.

So why did she appeal to me so much?

Leftover Tom

You don't often see perfectly matched quirks among couples, but Mr. Wonderful and I happen to have identical appetites for strange secondhand stuff. Our funky taste in rerun treasure swung schizophrenically between curbside refuse and head-scratching antiquities, all the better if it was battered, broken, quite ugly, or completely useless. No surprise, then, for us to walk away from an exceedingly eccentric sell-all with piles of orchid-growing gear, crippled candelabras, and menacing Medieval-ish weaponry-as-wall-art—all wrapped in cobwebs and decades of dust, straight off the Addams Family set.

And while a dose of thrift vaccinated Chips from most pedestrian temptations, he was, in fact, wide open to a monumental budget in the name of adventure, romance, or karmic inevitability.

Like a spur-of-the-moment buying spree on a new house.

On our street, on the corner was an amazing Daliesque house with Spanish architecture. It was crazy, crazy beautiful. And then it was for sale.

I called Chips at work. "You have to come home right now," I told him. "They're having an estate sale at the Spanish house."

Chips was amused by my persistent pleas. "They'll run all weekend. I can go on Saturday."

"No, the *house* is for sale!"

Chips, my fearless warrior, immediately raced to my side. We walked into the house. We bought the house. Then we sold our house. In all of three weeks, we were ensconced.

As was, it turned out, a squatter on our new property.

Our new hacienda had its own subterranean grotto, complete with store-bought stalactites; an old servant's quarters, now taken over by a standing army of vermin; the skeletal remains of greenhouses ensnarled in a forest of poison oak; and a cat.

Leftover Tom, my nickname for him, was a raggedy orange-on-white ruffian, who was none too happy with my garrulous greeting. He returned it with a withering *what the hell* glare, then vanished into the privacy of his alley. Yes, it was *his*; he let me know with a sauntering strut, declaring dominion over our back block.

I worried for him, in spite of his first-rate Buddha belly. It was the stirring of my then-tepid furry noblesse oblige, my clueless animal days before strays came to stay. I wasn't looking out for love; I was looking out for his life. Cats were not, in that environment, capable of living on their own. The raccoons would kill them, the dogs would kill them, they would starve, or they would get hit by cars. I was unwilling to leave him in the world he'd been occupying. It did not work for me.

So I satisfied myself with daily non-rat rations dispensed near his favored escape path. Every day I provided for him, but weeks passed, and my hands-off hobo hadn't budged one paw. He wouldn't even offer me a measly good-morning blink. This was one tough dude. Everything was on his *take-it-or-leave-it* terms, strictly MYOB (though he wasn't too proud to snatch a few of my grab-and-go tidbits). He did well for himself with his own culinary skills: plumped songbirds, burger-sized bugs, and the Thursday-night all-you-can-eat smorgasbord of garbage goodies, all quenched with a poolside chlorine-tini.

He was a whirlwind, especially in hot pursuit of a rotund rodent, whose fate I tried to ignore. Though I admit to a squeamish sympathy for the pest, I was nonetheless grateful our new feline friend's decisive actions would un-invite the rat and his cousins from their erstwhile accommodations among us. I was transfixed with the cat's cheetah speed and flying paws. He was a spine-chilling killing machine.

Over time, our skittish tenant mapped out a buffer between us, eliminating his need to flee at the first hint of the gabby Lunch Lady. Conversations, however, remained one-sided; my monologues earned me only his blank stare. But somehow, on some seriously subliminal whiskery wavelength, I felt a flimsy thread of communion take hold. After months of babbling sweet endearments and dropping off table scrap (one more useful than the other, I'm sure), a breakthrough! On that fateful evening, I had wandered out for some fresh air and moonlight. Suddenly, my painfully shy alley cat approached. He planted himself within slashing distance of my feet. I had to snap shut my shock-and-awe jaw! Slowly, I crouched down to face my foe, all the while mumbling cocktail pleasantries. It was a bold move on my part, but he took it in stride. It turned out *I* was the one who did not take it in stride, not when I saw the nasty new gash on my new buddy's already-well-gashed ear. ER urgency overruled self-preservation on the part of both parties, so I scooped up my once-paranoid, now-docile patient. I carried him into the guest room and into the good life.

Oh, the speechless surprise on Chips's face when he found our incorrigible alley cat demurely nestled into a wingback chair as if born to the manor! To be frank, Mr. Wonderful did not have the most wonderful reaction. He was far from thrilled about another addition to the domestic ranks. We already had Daisy Mae, a naughty mutt I brought into our marriage (love me, love my dog), and our cats, Lil'Abner and Hoover, plus Mr. Jimmy Mittens Jr., my very first fuzzy salvage, the kitten from the gym. And now here he was, another mouth to feed. Another troublemaker threatening to drive one more whiskery wedge between Mr. Wonderful and his fur-brained bride.

To be fair, the dust settled quickly. With some benevolent bargaining, a deal was sealed, allowing only limited membership privileges for our lowly enlistee. He was rechristened Irish (what else to call a redheaded tom?) and was made to bunk in Daisy's laundry-room boudoir. Daisy, I confess, was not thrilled with her new roommate, despite the interloper's awkward attempts at cross-critter camaraderie. His days were his own—sort of. He was no longer king of the jungle, nor a gladiator thirsting for blood. Instead, he perused his former hunting grounds from a labyrinth of customized cat corrals that Chips had built for him. Irish, in essence, had a private park with a jogging path, posh poolside views, a plethora of discreet sunbathing terraces, and a fully furnished cat cabana beneath the cool canopy of an overgrown plum tree—though truth be told, it was rarely used by our rugged outdoorsman. He did, however, approve of the rest of his convoluted Rube Goldberg maze of chicken wire, lawn, limbs, and lumber. He made that obvious each morning by his frantic fifty-yard dash directly into his personal playground. And his stubborn sit-in at day's end. Enough that both bribery and broomsticks got involved to get him back inside.

Having taken the great leap forward into polite society, Irish lapped up all my strange smooching like a seasoned will-purr-for-Purina pro. But he still wore his large, round scalping wound in all its gory glory. No tabby tonic could fill in that cranial crater.

Then one day, he just stopped eating.

Cats are notorious super-survivors, so when your tiny tiger's appetite disappears, chances are that Fluffy's about to give up one of those fabled nine lives. But I was unwilling to bid my hard-won friend farewell just as he'd blossomed into pethood, so I revived my haggard boy with chicken broth drop by ever-so-slow drop. Chemically cured or simply loved back to life, he shook off death with catly je ne sais quoi.

Back on all fours, Irish won whole-house-cat privileges from Chips in practically no time—those sly little negotiators always worm their way onto the least likely of laps. Irish's unrivaled reputation as a no-nonsense, one-strike-one-kill Terminator didn't hurt either (hasta la vista, vermin). For his able colleague Jimmy Mittens, a multitalented whole-house mouser, those were trying times. Mother Nature meandered in as she pleased through wall-to-wall cracks, holes, and gaps. English ivy wandered along broken windowpanes, morphing from garden groundcover to growing wallpaper (strangely charming, in a *Little Shop of Horrors* sort of way).

But football-sized Norway rats, marauding Vikings of the rodent world, had invaded our vast, ungoverned attic, industriously pillaging and plundering through the nights. Those big, bad dudes were way above our plucky seven-pound pouncer's pay grade—forget about our other cats, the pair of pretty little pleasure killers, both blue bloods and strictly part-time dabblers in paw-and-jaw-powered death.

And all best human efforts hardly made a dent in the horrible herd. Chips tried patio vigils, sharpshooting the dinner crowd at our bird (and beast) feeder, to no avail, and we made one very foolish foray into rat candy. Our nibblers would have no part of it, but leave it to our pup Daisy, known to ingest anything and everything remotely edible, to get herself a stomach pumping when we feared she'd stumbled upon the treats during her insatiable snacking sorties.

Oh, we were up against the best. Erik the Long-Tailed, a worthy specimen to be sure, among his Scandinavian subculture, had the audacity to challenge my authority from atop an open pantry door. Brazen and mocking, he was utterly unimpressed by the horrified hundred-and-plenty-pound human frozen in her tracks. He had the gall to stroll back into his well-stocked pantry without a backward glance!

My braver half would have none of that cheek. He drafted a surefire game plan. He would call in the heavy artillery.

Enter our war hero, Irish the Great Squeak Slayer. Chips recalled the seasoned battle veteran to active duty, rousting him from daily doze number seventeen and stationing him at the front line. With Irish in position, Chips opened the pantry door. Irish turned his warrior eye to a blockading case of Quaker Oats, silently signaling First Officer Chips for its removal. This accomplished, Erik the Doomed bolted directly into waiting paws. With masterful maneuvers, Irish bit and shook the frantic varmint, finally bringing him *down*. Erik the Doomed was Erik the Dead.

Irish, in humble soldier fashion, politely submitted to a shower of praise with a *what, really? It's kitten play* glance of bemusement. He did, however, appreciate his instant promotion to Most Favored Bedmate.

He remained our hero, holding couch-potato court with all the charm of truly superior beings, but even the noblest among us must leave before we're ready to say goodbye. By then a rumpled old retiree, Irish saw out his closing hours in the warm, sunny corners of our home. By then, we'd accumulated a dozen other high-maintenance lowlifes underfoot, but still, our fur-clogged house felt empty. A century of cat years later, my heart still pined for that purring Prince Charming.

My equivalent cat sorrow was Simon, one of the barn cats we'd scooped up as kittens. Long past the age of eighteen, and with his brother Sebastian departed a year earlier, Simon too closed out his hours in a warm patch of sun.

Was that it? Was that our commonality? That I simply cared for my cat, as did Betsy? We often look for ways to relate to those around us—oh, you're Dutch, too? You had a cinderblock dorm at university as well? You like summer best, like me? It's *a* connection, but that answer seemed somewhat superficial for my growing interest.

For my growing admiration.

And now, I wondered if I was getting somewhere. I admired Betsy's perseverance, her tenaciousness, her (ahem) doggedness. If I had found a foul-tempered feline in my new backyard, I would have fled with a prance of dismissal. ***If he doesn't want my help, then*** fine*!* Yet Betsy returned day after day, week after week, never giving up on her good intentions.

It reminded me, strangely, of a former student of mine.

Aaron, a grade 11 student, was on the autism spectrum. Though he was high functioning, Aaron would often lash out in anger, unable to control his frustrations. He was never violent, nor did he alienate the other students in the class; his wrath was directed toward me. I understood his reactions were not personal, even as he told me, often, to fuck off. I knew he was hurting, and I just wanted to help. Aaron, unlike an alley cat, had a support system; it wasn't just me in his corner at school, but still he struggled. Day in, day out. Some days were better; some not so much. But I kept trying. I was no saint. It took a great deal of patience and deep breathing, and I admit I snapped at him a time or two more than I should have. Despite my every effort at empathy, he remained a trying student.

Until one day he didn't.

One day he came into class, like normal, but instead of taking his seat, he came over to me, awkward and unsure. "I'm sorry, Ms. Braaksma," he said, his eyes on the ground. That was it. He did not explain for what specifically he was apologizing, nor did it matter.

"Thank you, Aaron."

It was a breakthrough. From that moment on, Aaron tried hard to regulate his emotions. He was successful some days and not others, but we'd come to a sort of peace between us. I was not the miracle worker in Aaron's life; I was but one adult trying to do right by him for the seventy-five minutes a day that I saw him. But I had tried, and tried again, and I kept trying, and that was my whole philosophy, my passion, my raison d'être in the classroom, to keep trying to reach out to my students. They were, like Betsy's cats, out there fighting, trying to survive in the only ways they knew how, and like Betsy, I just wanted to make their lives a little bit easier.

Was I, then, in Betsy's stories, seeing myself?

Chapter 4

When I was in middle school, I was a bully. I wouldn't have labeled myself as such at the time, of course, but hindsight is perfect vision, right? Except the childlike ideas I had of bullies—mean boys beating up weak boys on the playground—did not fit my self-image, neither then nor as I got older. But we've come a long way in understanding bullying; it's not necessarily about physical violence, nor overt taunting. No, my friends and I were stealth in our cruelties. I made new friends in grade 6, our first year of a new middle school, and of those, there was one girl, Tammy, who had tagged along from my new friends' old elementary school. I didn't hate Tammy, but nor did I particularly like her. She was . . . different. Isn't that the excuse we all use when we're cruel to others? At eleven, I didn't understand what was different about her—or why my own reactions were so, so wrong. Instead, all I knew was that I found it hard to be around her. She was there, among my new group of friends. All. The. Time.

I told myself I could take her in small doses, so when I'd had enough, I would walk away. Only, it wasn't just me. Our whole group excluded Tammy. But then time would wane, and we'd decide we needed another person for our game, and we called Tammy back. She'd eagerly join us . . . until we got tired of her presence yet again. Sometimes I was ringleader, sometimes I was meek follower, but never, not once, did I think of how much we were hurting Tammy. And, oh, our hypocrisy! Because Tammy would invite us to her birthday parties, and we'd all go. And because all our parents thought she was part of our group, she, too, was invited to all of ours. She was one of us. Except when we decided she wasn't.

I moved away in grade 8; our group lost touch and I haven't seen her since. As the years passed, as I grew older and wiser, I grew much more repentant. I'd prided myself on being *nice*, yet how could I have done that to Tammy? Kids can be cruel, and as an adult, I had to own up to that. Even if I'd been nice ever since, I still had to acknowledge what I had done as a kid. And recognizing that I *had* been capable of such insensitivity at one point made me feel very . . . human.

Betsy, on the other hand, seemed superhuman. A saint, an angel. So no, given my own flawed history, perhaps I was wrong after all. Perhaps, in Betsy's stories, I could see nothing of myself and everything of her strength of character, love, and goodness.

The Cat House

Before our Dallas days ended, Fate, the celestial card shuffler it was, determined my path would cross with a reclusive old neighbor, tucked away in her own parallel universe. Mildred was cloistered within two tangled acres of Amazonian overgrowth (nothing short of a well-oiled chainsaw could navigate beyond that front walk) not far from our house. There was nothing but a gravel-and-dirt winding driveway that we could see from the street; whatever lay beyond was hidden. Chips had lived here long before me, and even he had no idea who lived there.

I was determined to find out, so I walked down the path, up to the house, and introduced myself. Mildred was single and had been her whole life. She had retreated from the outside world, unwilling to face—or have the rest of us face—the stares and squeamish stomachs brought about by her own horribly ravaged face, half gone from cancer she had chosen not to treat. It wasn't a death disease; instead, it ate away at her face. Mildred would wear bandages to cover her face, but still she was self-conscious. When I learned that she shared my open-pet-door policy, I refused to accept her social reluctance. Our shared love of animals would trump her discomfort, and soon a friendship was born over sugar cookies and cats.

And geese, and raccoons and pigeons, and, well, almost every manner of down-on-their-luck critters in Mildred's Ark. There was the cantankerous goose salvaged from some objectionable amateur-aviary situation; the blind and one-footed pigeons; every last raccoon on the block (now too fat—and way too friendly—from their nightly all-you-can-eat backyard buffet). But the main event was cats, cats, and more cats, sprawled out in siestas on every spare surface of her threadbare home and lurking within feline-fantasy jungle gardens.

Our cat-crazy coffee klatches carried on until Mildred could no longer keep up the daily zookeeper's grind. The house was becoming dilapidated. Something had to give. My broken-down and heartbroken friend finally gave the green light to reduce her animal inventory. Her goose, bad-boy Big Bird that he was, mean and messy, retired among floating friends-of-a-feather, a fabulous swan song for the beast. We helped clear out the backyard banditos—ten raccoons, at least, who didn't always stay in the backyard and would boldly invade Mildred's front parlor when she was too weak to fight. Mr. and Mrs. Missing-Parts Pigeon both met their maker.

That left a dwindling ragbag of tattered old cats (straight out of an Andrew Lloyd Webber casting call). There were six of them. They were all she had left to love, her lone reason to get out of bed every morning, the last threads of an unraveling life.

At the same time, Chips and I were planning to move to our very own Mayberry. I couldn't leave my failing friend to her fate, though. I had to convince her to move into a nursing home. She was close to the people in her church, but truly, not even with their help could she take care of herself any longer. It was then that I made a soul sister's pact:

"If you go, I'll take the cats."

Adoption for her twenty-four-legged tribe anywhere else would have been impossible, not with this hoard of high-maintenance mongrels.

And so, the great Cat Deal was sealed. It was with a lead-weighted heart that Mildred said farewell to the last of her dearly beloved, though for me, there was bittersweet relief. I was grateful my offer of kitty custody would enable Mildred to get the care she needed, but sad, sad, sad that they had to be separated. Still, it was for the best as I rounded up Big Tex, Maggie, Blackie, Sunny, Bunny, and Blue and headed to Carthage, Missouri.

Of course, halfway through that teeth-clenching six-hour (seemed like sixty) road trip, I wondered what I had done. The howl-a-thon alone of Confused Cat Blues was enough to drive me crazy!

We had room for them in our new place. We'd moved into a three-story house, where the third story was finished but not in use. The stairs to the third floor were closed off by a door, so the cats could easily be contained up there. There was also a separate bedroom that had been a maid's quarter, so with one great big open room with a vaulted ceiling and one bedroom, they would have lots of space.

The six of them hit the ground like gypsies in that third-floor feline flophouse, full of meow-worthy miscellany to mix and mingle among, with unlimited clawing and camping privileges on the bachelor-pad leftover furniture we'd moved in there.

Two of them panicked completely and disappeared. We had no idea where they had gone. Did they fall in a wall? Where did they go? It became a big undertaking to unearth the devilish creatures. It turned out one of them had burrowed into a small space in the highest rafter recesses, the last place we had thought to look. I grabbed the cat—now a wildcat, for she was fierce—and pitched her into the bedroom, slamming the door shut. The other cat had gotten herself above the bedroom; she'd scaled the wall and wasn't coming down for hell or high water. Until, that is, Mr. Wonderful's heroic high-wire extraction. She, too, went into the bedroom, though we would come to realize that Sunny was, in fact, not the lost little orange lamb we'd all assumed; she would turn out to be the Gray Whisker's Gang lead lioness, a real spitfire.

She'd just been lying low (lying high) while all the flying fur settled into their new junk-filled jungle.

With Bunny and Sunny settled (sort of), we still had to translate Maggie's screeching tirades—she was her own air-defense warning system—and we had to heal Blackie's chronic queasy nature. Not to mention managing the free-range potty for cowboy Tex (don't fence me-*ow* in), and expending futile efforts at grooming his gnarly coat. We finally had to resort to the local pet barber, and Tex returned home a trans-furred creature, a feline French poodle, if you will.

When Mom and Dad came to visit, mid–snowbird migration, there was no choice but to introduce them to the NASCAR (National Association for Six Cat Attic Racing) speedway now thundering over their second-floor bed. It seemed unlikely that the stealthy six-pound critters could be anything but silent as the grave, but Cat Rule #15 illustrated all laws of physics went out the window. They could raise a ruckus worthy of the Calgary Stampede.

It's not that my parents weren't accustomed to plenty of Pauly pet antics. They'd visited before with our own cats' blindly probing paws under occupied bathroom doors (nothing steams a cat like a lockout) or the nabbing of treasures from parked purses and grab-and-go groceries. Our dog, Daisy Mae, in fact, carried on a dangerous paper-money fetish in which she gulped down all the bills she could sink her terrible-terrier teeth into. No, they were used to our little vultures lying in wait for unguarded goodies, but our third-floor three-ring circus put us into a whole new nuthouse league.

And that was when we had only six extra cats.

It wasn't long before I noticed walkers on our street reverently pausing at our curb, their gaze directed upward toward our roof with frank fascination. Puffed up with pride, I thought they were admiring our home. I deflated quickly when one such gawker explained she was merely taking in our latest law-and-(dis)order lineup staring down at the passersby from the picture window in their lofty lair. Given how very far we'd gone beyond the town's ordinance's allotment of pets allowed, I envisioned my notoriety as the owner of the Home for Wayward Whiskers leading me to the county jail, unbecoming orange jumpsuit and all. The image suddenly stifled my silly urge to guide photo safaris of our wild kingdom. (Cat Rule #18: Attention, fellow hoarders! Never, ever whisper your furry head count!)

At first, it seemed our own little Mayberry was marvelously benign, with flower boxes and friendly smiles. We'd moved to a community where there were parades of cakes and casseroles for every bride, birth, bed spell, and bereavement. It was as if there were Hansel-and-Gretel gingerbread houses for homes and a Disney-castle courthouse keeping watch over its sleepy town square.

But underneath the illusion, there ran a steady stream of gossip, humor, wonder, and angst based on our box-of-chocolate assortment of cats. I was soon resigned to my new role as busybody fodder. *You have* how *many cats?* Or, *Why in heavens would you take in so many?*

Chips had had enough, however. One question too many provoked him to pen the following answers, ready-made for any intrusive interest:

1. *We have one cat by choice* [well, just a little old-math/ new-math/he-said/she-said semantics technicality], *plus Jimmy, a former stray* [our lone surviving charter house-mouser at that time].
2. *We have a family of secondhand ex–alley cats, from Betsy's ailing friend, Mildred.*
3. *We have a floating number of foster cats—still more alley salvage—available for adoption, now boarding with us because no one else bothered to get them off the mean streets.*
4. *The number of cats in our home is not our preference (two would be plenty* [I'll second that]*) but, rather, a sad commentary that only a small minority of people find it unacceptable to ignore a domestic animal that is abandoned, hungry, cold, wet, wounded, sick, and suffering.* [Dayyum!]

Chips goes on to ask a few questions of his own:

1. *Are you a compassionate person?*
2. *If so, how many strays have you taken in? If you feel it wouldn't be convenient to have surplus animals camping at your house, please recognize that it's rarely convenient for us.*
3. *Since it wouldn't work for you to bring them home, how many spare cats have you taken to the local shelter?* [And this concludes the Q&A portion of Mr. Pissed-Off Pauly's MYOFB smackdown!]

My knight in shining armor carried plenty of those sizzling slips in his wallet, distributing as needed with only a punctuating glare of incrimination. That little scrap of paper could pack a huge wallop, silencing even the nosiest nail-biters on the spot.

Chips was right, though. It wasn't easy to adjust to this new compassion-for-creatures lifestyle. We had a Grand Pauly Plan but it dissipated on contact with, well, fur. Our budgets—blown. Our buildings—bought, sold, and sliced every which way to accommodate current hairy-hotel hospitality. Our travel—nonexistent. Our focus on technology—my never-ending quest for the greatest litter box engineering. We were not just cook, butler, laundress, masseuse, and court jester for *one* cat; we bowed to more than half a dozen. How, I wanted to know, could a ham-sized critter wield such superhuman political power over our very own home's domestic policy and procedure? Most definitely we felt the weight (all right, ball and chain) of our zoological overcommitment.

But what is the point in complaining about the time and money spent on Mildred's many dear mayhem-makers? Or the growing paycheck-charring enterprise of fostering more and more stray cats? Whimpering and whining over life's little hiccups was so very un-Viking of me. If Great-Great-Great-(and so on and so forth) Grandpa Harold the Horrible could suck up the bubonic plague, an axe in the head, or running out of herring, then surely I, as a good Norse descendent, could swallow the apoplexy-inducing debit columns at the Pauly's Funny Farm.

Mildred lasted only a few months after her four-footed family farewells. She was welcomed at the Pearly Gates—through Gabriel's express lane, no doubt—long before Tex, Maggie, Blackie, Bunny, or Blue left this earth. In fact, ancient

Sunny, at twenty-three, and nearly toothless with a snowy snout, was the last living reminder of my Hercules-hearted old friend.

I check off everything I would have done differently had I been in Betsy's position:

- I would have never become determined to meet a reclusive, unknown neighbor. (I live in the country so I don't have to ***have*** neighbors!)
- Had I made it past the jungle-growth of a driveway, I would have faltered at Mildred's face. I'd love to think I'm better than that, but am I really?
- Had I had Betsy's decency to look beyond Mildred's outer scars and see the beauty of a human she was, I would have offered vaguely to "let me know if there's anything I can do to help."
- Had I indeed been able to follow through with meaningful help, I would ***not*** have agreed to *six* cats!

So yes, it seemed as if Betsy was beyond me. She demonstrated a compassion, integrity, and sacrifice I could only admire, if not replicate. I was in awe of her kindness and her determination.

Chips laughed when I told him how Betsy came across as a humble hero. He didn't deny her amazing efforts or incredible impact, but he—and another of Betsy's stories—set me straight about her true, imperfect, short-tempered sass.

Which, of course, made me love her more.

Chapter 5

"Betsy saw them when no one else did," Chips explained about the animals Betsy took in. "But people often had the mistaken impression that Betsy ***wanted*** to do this, that she liked to do this. They would call her and say—and they'd only do this once, by the way—they'd say, 'Betsy, I was just going to the grocery store, and I saw there was a stray cat at the corner of Main and Third,' thinking Betsy would charge over there to get it. And Betsy's response would be 'Here's what you do. You come over here, I'll give you a Havahart kennel. You go back, you pick up the animal. You take it home, you give it some food and water, you take it down to the vet, have it checked out, make sure it's not diseased, make sure it gets its shots, get it ready for adoption, then you either adopt the animal out or you keep it or you take it to the humane society.' She made it clear you do not relieve yourself of responsibility, or think you're doing good trying to pass it off, like, ***Oh, gee, there's a stray dog and I told Betsy about it, so now I feel better about it.*** Betsy's assertion was clear: If you're going to feel good about yourself, you're going to do it. Otherwise, you've done nothing except continue the problem. She would say that to her friends, too. They may not go get it, but they wouldn't call a second time."

Chips continued, "Later, when we moved to Florida and we didn't see any stray cats, Betsy admitted she was tired of being a one-person humane society. It was an emotionally difficult thing to do. You bond to these animals. And they get sick and they die and you have to put them down and now you're going through cycles that aren't any fun. Some cats aren't people-animals. They want to be left alone. And of the cats that we had, there were only a few that were people-cats. Mostly they were just there. So when we no longer took in any more animals, I know it was a relief to her. It allowed her more time to do other things she enjoyed and she didn't have as much of a responsibility."

Betsy's stories are often light in tone, laced with good-hearted humor and affection. In all the dizzying escapes, Betsy laughs off the challenges; she doesn't dive too deeply into the dark, frustrating times of rescuing, fostering, and finding families for the strays. It would be easy to miss Chips's assessment in Betsy's stories alone.

If it weren't for her snark.

Suddenly, as I read more of Betsy's stories, I came to appreciate how so not perfect she truly was.

Chips described her as a take-charge personality. "She said she was very shy as a little girl and she decided to overcome that. We could walk into an event where we didn't know anyone. Betsy just charged up and introduced herself to people all over place and got to know a great number of people right away."

I could see that—her fervor obvious on the page—but what I also came to recognize was how little patience she often had for some of those very same people.

Real Housewives of Mayberry

The *idiotic* idea of abandoning a furry family member, turning loose your formerly adored and indulged—or at least tolerated—pet, is unjustifiably bad beyond all feeble excuses. And, oh, by the way, illegal coast to coast. How could anyone think their once-loved—or at least tolerated—pet could suddenly fend for itself? The animal would be fuzzy-brained (a whole new, strange, scary world!), tongue-tied (in the most symbolic cat-got-your-tongue scenario), and, oh, flat broke. I'm not clear how the humans who abandon their pets think that Fluffy could waltz into Walmart and grab a few cans of Friskies in all her favorite flavors. You know, the way she was *used* to getting food. Out of a can. By humans. *Not* foraging in dumpsters and alleys or out in the wild.

It's true that the really twisted Satan-and-associates stuff makes the six o'clock news, and of course that makes my blood boil. *Step up, Meathead; at least give your cat a fighting chance at the nearest furball flophouse called a shelter!* But it seems like the lion's share of drop-and-drive sadism is fueled by plain old stupidity. (Probably fertilized in some way by all that nifty nine-lives mythology, which, by the way, is hogwash. Your cat really will die only once. That's it. Don't blow it.) People's stupidity truly boggles my mind. It's like the cranial headlights go out, leaving only some sort of blinding high beam in their brains. *It's a great idea to get rid of my critter!* Who *thinks* that? It boggles the mind, yet I have, sadly, seen it too many times, even among those who claim to have full control over their own minds. They may be compos mentis (though, are they really sane?), yet still they dump their pussycats. I am thinking, for example, of a pair of convenient Christian pseudo pals who casually announced—*casually* announced, and to *me*, of all people!—that they had redumped a mama and her latest litter in a rural area. And their reaction to my seething admonishments? (For yes, I was clear in my position about their idiocy.) Huffy surprise.

Another example: A swanky Mr. and Mrs. among the Mayberry Swell Set shamelessly admitted leaving behind their loyal lap-napper kitty simply because Minnie-Mouser hadn't been around on moving day. They speculated, without a wince, that one of their neighbors would probably pick up the cat slack.

Probably? Probably? *Probably??*

No matter the intensity of devotion to animal welfare, most halfway-civilized juris-*purr*dences still hand out at least a pittance of a wrist slap to the wallet for these crimes of neglect and abandonment. Some of the more fur-friendly lands also add in lockup for certain crimes. None, of course, come close to my fantasy justice: giving the creeps a nice, long taste of their own wicked medicine in some food-and-central-heat-free hinterlands. Still, the consequences of casting away kitty are often meagerly meted out. There's plenty of blame to go around: see-no-evil citizens, cop-a-plea prosecutors, tiptoeing-to-reelection judges. I get it; it's coin-operated politics as usual. Since Kitty's got no cash, Kitty's got no clout.

But the Mayberry population who were predisposed to dispose of their pets in our over-littered little town were about to receive a blunt primer about the hazards of giving poor Puss the old heave-ho. And all at the hands of my otherwise cool-as-a-cucumber, live-and-let-live Mr. Wonderful.

We were entertaining friends from Dallas, soaking up the sun on our wisteria-covered porch after hauling our city-slicker buddies around Mayberry's hotspots, when Chips showed up at a full boil, cursing a deep blue streak. Considering he's a real smooth operator, his feathers were *really* ruffled. In his hands was a powderpuff of wiggling fluff. The poor creature had obviously been deposited in our yard by some cowardly creep; the teensy-weensy kitty couldn't run ten inches, let alone trot around the neighborhood. We were on our feet in an instant, scouting the crime scene. Two more copycat-kittens peeked out from the top of a cardboard box, parked illegally in our sugar snap pea plot. And even more appeared! Three more kittens were making a run for it, albeit at the tempo of a tortoise. My tough-enough guy was seeing red. It was a sight to behold as he ran out of expletives, especially since he was so tenderly juggling that squirming mass of fur. But in time, Chips's apoplexy diminished to PG grumbles by the sight of those half dozen kitty clowns tumbling about their new makeshift playpen. They were oblivious to the day's dark beginnings, flopping about without a care in the world, an admirable feline philosophy. Carpe diem for cats: mouse, milk, and be merry!

They may not have had a care in the world, but we most certainly did. We were in a panic over a potential plague of unwanted fleas infecting our own cats, though the two groups were separated. So instead of postponing a wet-pet wrestling contest, we dove right into a baptism-by-bathtub for the featherweight fleabags. After all, what were two puny pounds of roly-poly naivete to our savvy sensibilities and brute biceps?

Answer: One pocket-sized cat versus two towering humans turned out to be a pretty even match. We, the weary spa attendants, were soaked, slashed, and wiped out in that marathon of a six-kitty free-for-all. Our nemeses, none the worse for their baths, scampered right back to playtime.

Chips sprawled out in good-humored defeat. The winning army of squeaky-clean cats clamored all over him. There was photographic evidence of their victory. And in that delicious moment, two absolute certainties emerged: One, those irresistible imps would not be long under our roof, given how people-curious and people-comfortable they were; and two, beneath all that gruff man-of-steel stuff, I was married to a great big fur-coated marshmallow.

Clearly the dastardly dumbasses who had disposed of the six-pack of kitties had gotten wind of our soup kitchen for cats. They must have cased the joint for just the right drop-off moment. The timing of their appearance coincided much too neatly with our brief outing that morning. Beyond the obvious cruelty, what flummoxed Chips the most was the gall that would have propelled some deadbeat cat-dad to pawn off the kittens to us as if they were disposable trash. Normally Chips is a turn-the-other-cheek kind of guy, a paragon of patience, facing the foibles of friends, family, and (thank God) his fur-brained wife with great equanimity. But this villainous shoebox drop must have touched a nerve. There, in front of me, was No More Mr. Nice Guy. His inner Viking welled up, hell-bent on half-pint justice.

My valiant (ahem) *Purry* Mason detective dug into some kitty-ditcher clues. He turned up a big break. An alien auto was seen loitering suspiciously on the afternoon in question. With that solid lead, and the bemused cooperation of our Barney Fife–bored police force (those flashing cherries don't get much use in thug-free Mayberry), Chips tightened his dragnet. He took out a front-page *Wanted—ALIVE* ad in our local press, broadcasting the crime and the cunning culprit's getaway car. He sweetened the pot with a handsome reward for fingering the evildoer.

Yet sadly, despite all the pavement pounding and puzzle-piecing in our very own episode of *Law and Order: Special Little Victims Unit,* the Carton-O'-Kittens case was never cracked. Still, it was the talk of the town, and I don't doubt the guilty party lost sleep and treaded quite carefully in their notorious navy minivan. If nothing else, at least other would-be tabby tossers were officially put on notice. Chips made it clear that such bad behavior was way beyond the pale and that they, too, would be hunted down by my livid lawyer-husband. It worked. We were never again the backyard bullseye of four-legged refuse. More importantly, I'm pretty sure all of Mayberry benefitted from my superhero honey's very public display of pet principles.

Meanwhile, a superfluous bit of sprucing up brought our sextuplets to the top of their game. In that hook-line-and-sinker state of kittenhood (the crack cocaine of critters—cheap, plentiful, and 100 percent addictive), our cuddly little rock stars created quite a stir among gaga groupies-to-be. In fact, three hopelessly infatuated families went home with twice what they had bargained for, a double dose of guaranteed fuzzball fun.

Our real-life Mayberry holds within the generally genteel populous a colorful cast of characters. We have the homogenously DNA'd hillbillies ("kissin' cousins" are a real thing in the Ozarks), the PhD gossipmongers, and even our very own fussbudget of a barber (no cuts for the politically incompatible). At first, Lawyer Pauly and his wife were quickly pegged to fit in the milquetoast mainstream, but I suspect it wasn't long before I was placed on a fence. No one quite knew what to do with me. How to categorize a sushi-and-fake-bacon-loving oddball marching miles off Main Street to a mighty different drum?

But early on (still under that attractive veil of anywhere-but-here exoticism), I was politely ushered into the Garden Club (the front-parlor bastion of primly pantyhosed Aunt Beas), the Book Club (beckoning footnote-craving Helen Crumps), and the Historic Preservation Auxiliary (the undisputed epicenter of matronly do-gooding). And so, I broke out my best Spanx—we're talking pinkies-up, doilies-down sweet tea and small talk (both dry as the Sahara, but for our bohemian literati, wherein language *and* liquor are known to flow freely)—and joined in all the frothy, frilly, estrogen-flooded fun.

What must those good women have thought, hearing that their newest *Real Housewives of Mayberry* recruit was often sprawled out next to a roadside drainage pipe in all manner of unladylike dishevelment, talking to herself and, apparently, to the pipe? I suspected there was some serious second-guessing among my wide-eyed sponsors, wondering if a bit more background work might have been in order before welcoming such a cuckoo into their finely feathered flock. I admitted to some fancy footwork to keep my foot out of my mouth, keeping a tight lid on my hatred of the hideous fur trade (Mayberry's country club crowd sported more dead animal skins per capita than traditional Inuit used to) and my one-drumstick-shy-of-meatless menu (culinary blasphemy deep in the heart of cow country). I understood the need for sugarcoated diplomacy in such a snug little fishbowl.

But rescuing kitties from the hard-knocks life—my number one job assignment from God—didn't always fly under the Regular Folks radar. Fortunately, I knew how to ride Chips's wide—and unquestionably sane—coattails, which cut me, the semiweird wife, some slack in spite of my assorted loose screws.

Still, my notoriety as the Nutcase for Fleabags led to unintended consequences. People did want to talk to me—if I could help them sort out their critter conundrums. *Miss Minxie's got another basket of buns in the oven?* I'd be lecturing on Spaying for Simpletons, or Neutering for Nitwits. *You just don't feel like taking Fido with you when you move?* Newsflash: Friends don't leave best friends behind. *You found a stray cat?* Congratulations! It's not coming here; the Pauly hairball hotel has no vacancies; we manage to find our guests quite well on our own, thank you very much. But let me give you the Timid Tabby Roundup Rundown.

I was, it seemed, a hands-free hotline for every awkward animal occasion, walking everyone through the furry detritus into the land of rainbows and kittens and happily ever afters.

Of course, as soon as rules are made, they are easily broken. I had thought I was hard and fast on my help-*yourself*-to-strays dictate, but yes, once again, I was snookered into someone else's *cat*astrophe. My practically perfect pal Sally had bought into all my proselytizing, no great surprise, given the broken-record messiah that I was. So, when we had gathered one night for a lively literary chat to dissect that month's juicy tome, Sally reported her discovery of a cute little kitty hanging out in a culvert mere paws—*ahem,* feet—away from a menacing motorway skirting our metropolis. She announced this to all of us present, yet of course she aimed her carefully prepared remarks at my tabby-tuned ears. The Book Club was my favorite of the Mayberry bunch; it was a brain-fertilizing Oprah-fest with a flavorful age range, from newlyweds to empty-nesters, a mix of bank accounts, minimum to magnificent, and a diversity of philosophies, from Baptist to Buddhist.

I sighed as all eyes turned to me. Sally was as subtle as a cement truck. She knew she'd hit bullseye. I, her go-to pet catcher, would be propelled to the perilous pipe.

The next day, I planted myself in front of that drain pipe and got a peek at the tiny squatter, crouched deep inside its bunker.

Its mama stared back at me with a shredding look as subtle as Sally's. *I'll slice you from stem to stern,* it said.

I was very good, by this time, at reading Cat.

She was a tough customer, this mama. She had a me(*ow*)-against-the-world skepticism (for good reason) that made her turn up her nose at my usual hostess gifts. She would not come quietly. By the end of my day's efforts, I'd garnered plenty of neck-craning gapes from bemused passersby and musical honks from chortling cars. (In support or mockery? One could never know, but was there harm in believing the best in people?) I'd garnered a sore bottom. I'd garnered a plethora of patience.

I'd garnered no cat.

Round Two of my feline-fetching finesses produced only ongoing amusement for my passing audiences. It was time to break out the heavy equipment. I dragged out my high-milage Havahart animal trap. I had to use it sparingly in multicat roundups, given that a second cat tended to avoid the box that had propelled a first cat into her *cat*aclysmic fate. The trap was, therefore, the cat nabber of last resort.

We were at the last resort.

Dutifully, I baited my mechanical critter-eater in the hush of dusk and settled down to my surveillance. I didn't have to wait long before a hungry little half-pint made a beeline for those easy pickings. Of course, I had little hope for an easy double play. The rookie was in the cage; Mama, a team veteran, was not so easily fooled. No surprise, then, that street-seasoned Mama had evaporated into the night.

I tried to look at the bright side; her little baby ball of fur was off the mean streets. And Mama was clearly wise in the ways of her tough world, so she'd be okay. Of course, she'd be barefoot and pregnant before long and again and again for the duration of her fertile days. It broke my heart to think of her endless entrapment in that bio-*illogical* baby-making cycle—and of course all those mini-mousers, like the little kitty I'd just rescued, deluging the streets of Mayberry. It is a feline fallout ad infinitum.

So I returned at breakfast, by which time Mama had reclaimed that basement culvert, nonchalantly blinking *good morning* from her concrete foyer as if she'd invited me over for coffee and field-mouse muffins. Either unaware of my culpability in the kit-napping or thinking I'd somehow regurgitate her vanished girl, she serenely received my social call (no doubt confident of her superior pipe-diving dash). I pulled out a ten-pounder travel kennel and a quarter pound of dolphin-safe deal sealer (standard Crazy Cat Lady car content). It was my portable prison, plan B, and I kept it discreetly behind me. I dropped down to cat's-eye level, purred out propaganda, and prattled on about her darling daughter. I elaborated on her kitten's white-mitten manners: a straight-A student for leaving it all in the litter box and a whisker-licking member of the clean-plate club. Mama leaned in for a closer listen. Whether she was curious about my singsong mumbo jumbo or (more likely) salivating at the odiferous bribe at hand, she was getting hooked. I had hope for a fur-bright finale.

And then! At this delicate juncture, a sad old sedan pulled into the parking lot behind me, maneuvering to get a closer look at our Dr. Dolittle melodrama. It took all my control to fight my cranky flare-up. I had to count to ten before I could even return their hello.

"Whatcha doin'?" a boy asked as he hung both arms out the rear window.

How shocked was I when Mama Cat didn't bat an eye!

"It's an interspecies standoff," I said.

The kid was intrigued, so he stuck around as I mapped out my plan. We settled into our vigil, a part of me hoping I was planting a be-kind-to-kitties seed in this youth. He was not exactly quiet, especially commenting at the slightest twitch of Tunnel Tabby's tail, but much to my amazement, Mama was not the least put off by her new cheerleader. (One of my few rock-solid rules in life: Never, ever bet against a cat.)

Mama Cat inched closer. So did I. I faked ho-hum yawns and my best couldn't-care-less pantomime, but all the while I was worming my way toward her with all the stealth my aching bum could muster. We slowly came together. Finally, having gathered enough do-it-*now*! nerve (and losing the last of my artificially implanted patience), I grabbed the unsuspecting cat and plunked her into my plastic Cinderella carriage. A Hail-Mary hollering broke out among the peanut gallery, now expanded from just one kid, as Mama rammed her jail walls.

Mama Cat and I wished our fan club a fond farewell. (Well, *I* did; Mama would have used other f-words, if she could have spoken our language.) It was a good reminder to rein in my shamefully short fuse; in this case patience had won out.

I am happy to report that ultimately, my la-di-da membership privileges in Mayberry's High Society were never rescinded—despite the raised eyebrows and head scratches at the mounting evidence of my apparent cat-induced insanity. It's funny, what I learned about small-town life. Yes, it's a pretty tight social squeeze for free spirits and fenceless minds, but it's also, in some ways, an example of acceptance. When tempers simmer and tongues slow their wagging, the mainstream tend to offer us Fringe Elements a certain "don't ask, don't tell" tolerance. And so, joining Mayberry's other kooky bit players, this Stray Lady goes about her alleyway business scrounging up leftover cats.

I've never been to Carthage, Missouri—Betsy's Mayberry—but I picture myself there, with Betsy, at her book club. I imagine her practically perfect pal Sally, who would have hosted the event in her practically perfect house. I'd come as a friend of Betsy's, so despite my tinge of jealousy that Sally gets the "practically perfect pal" label, I'd be welcomed into her home. Betsy would have prepared me for the event. She would have dished on all the people who were coming, each of the Aunt Bees and the docile newlyweds, and even the fringe element—including details of how they each qualified for their categories. I'd know who was in the Garden Club and who ***not*** to mention the Historical Preservation Auxiliary to since (I imagine) there might have been some sort of kerfuffle with the last meeting's agenda, and we wouldn't want to dive into troubled waters as we devoured our book of the month. I would have read it, of course. I imagine Betsy would have alerted me to the book choice before I arrived for my visit, and given that books are my life, I'd be excited to participate. I imagine it would have been a book I hadn't yet read (an easy feat, despite my voracious reading habit, given the tsunami of books published every year and a flood of good ones, at that). I imagine I'd have very much enjoyed the book, though as a professional in the industry, I'd no doubt find things to critique. Even so, I'd walk into Sally's house with the intent to remain quiet as a mouse. I would want to observe, not just the fine ladies of Mayberry but also Betsy "in the wild." I imagine we'd gotten to know each other well before this scene; I imagine Betsy would have let me in on the dirt and her predictions about how it would all go down. The book club was Betsy's favorite, too, so she would tell me she'd be relaxed and amused, instead of on guard.

Sally's house would be a fine old Victorian home, three stories, reminiscent of a fairy tale. There would, naturally, be a white picket fence, with gorgeous gardens and a clean, well-swept stone path. Inside, her house, with the original hardwood, refinished, would ooze warmth and charm.

We would sit in her living room, adorned with modern furniture, a deep gray suede couch, patterned wingbacks, and some thick dining room chairs brought in to round out the circle. Betsy would take one of those; she'd leave the more comfortable furniture for the others. I knew she didn't drink much, but she'd accept a glass of wine, though she would be much too animated by the time Sally surreptitiously steered the conversation to the kitty to actually drink much.

"I saw a poor kitten by that old culvert near the highway," Sally would oh-so-casually mention.

I would see Betsy stiffen, and I, too, would cock my head, alert to the impending diatribe. I would have known of Sally; I would have known that ***Sally*** knew all about Betsy's penchant for ***not*** taking on other people's stray-pet problems, so I would have been surprised when Betsy would have sighed, her resignation pierced with determination.

My eyebrows would have shot up; I would have turned to Betsy with a wide-eyed gaze.

"Rules are made to be broken," she would have shrugged, a sly smile on her lips. "Oh, and you're coming with me, Jen."

Of course it's all a thread of fancy. Sally may actually live in an apartment or on a farm out of town, or in a double-wide trailer or in a mansion bigger than city hall. Betsy may not have had a glass of wine, may not have capitulated to Sally so quickly, may not have enjoyed the book under discussion that day. It's not, however, whether any of the details I spun in my head are right; it's that I enjoyed the notion that I could have been there, a friend of Betsy's, eager to be introduced to her world in person.

As with all fantasies, there is no basis in reality, especially harsh to appreciate when it's because the person is no longer with us, but it was nevertheless the power of Betsy's stories that fueled my imagination. It didn't matter whether I was anywhere close to right in the way I pictured the book-club scene. It mattered only that I was intrigued by Betsy's presence. She called herself part of the fringe element of her Mayberry, laughing at herself and her antics as much as anyone. She didn't take herself seriously, but she would move heaven and earth for her animals.

And she'd skewer anyone who dared dismiss the morality of her mission.

She had sass, and she had spunk, but she was far from perfect.

Yeah, my kind of friend.

Chapter 6

I've written a literary fantasy novel called the ***Fairy Tale Fringe Festival***. It features the Greek goddess Calliope, a Muse, who is banished to a magic island, where she creates a festival based on stories, myths, and legends. Actors, dancers, puppeteers, and storytellers of all kinds are welcome to share the joys of their tales. There is another protagonist, Fauna, a fiery storyteller, who comes to confront the brothers William and Jacob, Calliope's partners, who have more nefarious plans for the festival. In preparation, I read a lot of fairy tales and I read a lot ***about*** fairy tales. They're ubiquitous in our society—in every society—yet still, there's a sad stereotype that they are simply "children's stories." And that they all end happily ever after. Both are true yet also untrue. As a result of my research and writing, I am extra-attuned to ***any*** fairy tale reference. I feel a kinship with those who bring them up, especially adults. That is to say, I ***could*** feel a kinship with the millions who do, indeed, discuss fairy tales, but I ***do*** feel a kinship with those I actually encounter.

Which is why, before I'd read the first word of Betsy's next story, she'd graduated to my bosom buddy list. It didn't matter that she wasn't actually rewriting a fairy tale, only that she'd named two of her stray cats after fairy-tale characters. Close enough. She was kin.

Fairy Tails

Fairy-tale names belie the Brothers Grimm beginnings of our tag team kitties, Tinkerbell and Peter Pan. One had been wretchedly abandoned, tossed, like last year's flip-flops, by some sorry excuse for a family, and the other born to the mean streets. Both still carried the scars. The actions of abandonment may take but a minute, but the effects last for years. These two kittens were knee-jerk jittery, even among their select social circle (me and Chips as their two tiptoeing valets and the occasional saintly pet-sitter). They would vanish before any big, bad bogeyman visitor could lay evil eyes upon them. Tiny Tinkerbell had a manic *me, me, ME!* addiction to hands-on proof that her spot in the Pauly pecking order was secure, a sad holdover from her dark experiences with the dregs of human(un)kind. Peter Pan, on the other paw, hemmed and hawed his way around us like a lost little black panther that took a wrong turn at the last watering hole. I judged from his Boo Radley–bashful ways that young Pan had struggled to get by after moving from his mama's warm-and-fuzzy gutter. It had been, no doubt, a hardscrabble existence, a clear-cut hard time in the hood, which was cruelly unnatural given the many cozy millennia that cats have spent as well-fed and lap-warmed pets. Cats are considered domesticated animals for a reason.

Their tale began as Peter Pan alit late one evening, skulking from a streetlight's center-stage glare into the secret interior of a shrub. I followed (of course I did), and upon closer inspection, I found almond orbs glowing back at me. With a heavy sigh, for this stray-cat-rescue gig had sadly become a steady habit, I broke out my even-higher-mileage Havahart cage. It is a trap designed with a happy ending in mind. You simply insert one smelly can of StarKist tuna (the nectar of our surf-and-turf-addicted little gods), you keep an eye on its contents from a private-eye distance, then you wait for hunger's inevitable victory over even the cagiest alley cat caution. *Et voilà*! Another room reserved at Pauly's Halfway (to Lap Cat) House.

Peter Pan, as he would come to be known, was a gangly tween, all ears, legs, and tail, but he was no fool. He inhaled what was obviously his best (and most likely only) meal in a very long time with one eye skeptically glued to me. I wasn't a fool either, however. One slow-motion contented-cat blink gave me the sneak peek I needed to see a sweet soul hidden deep inside my newest protégé. Okay, perhaps I was a fool. That one blink did destroy my defenses and allowed unguarded optimism to set in. It was premature by even Pollyanna standards of irrational exuberance.

Tinkerbell turned up soon after. On my way to our Carnegie library with books to return, I'd passed a row of rickety old rent houses, which had been vacated ahead of bulldozing. On top of one swayback roof, casually perched, was a ten-pound tiger keeping a close eye on me. I reciprocated the surveillance. I easily lured Tom down with snacks and small talk, buttered him up with a back rub, and then popped him into my tomcat taxi before he knew what hit him. I was quite proud of my record-setting rescue; I could call it a day.

Or not.

As my new, perturbed prisoner tumbled about in his cell, another inquisitive eavesdropper approached. A tabby toddler, clearly the product of Tom's neighborly charms, skipped out from beneath one of the tenements on twinkle toes. And, goody gumdrops! Another pickup for our Lost Lil' Rascals ranch.

As one furry kitty usually leads to another, I flattened out for a peek in the crawl space beneath the porch and, sure enough, unearthed another baby Bengal, decked out in hypnotizing stripes and swirls just like his Don Juan of a daddy. Further in the cat cave was a dim hint of yet another cat crouched strategically beyond my reach, a tiny black-and-white sphinx keeping silent vigil over a kitten. I presumed she was Mama, though she was hardly bigger than her boy. I was tickled pink to spot an *I'm spoken for!* necklace around her scrawny little neck. It gave me rare hope for a happy purrer-to-person reunion. I easily rounded up her too-timid-to-touch kitten, but Mama (later to become Tinkerbell) stoically resisted the kitty caviar through luncheon and teatime. She was clearly onto my mechanical magic trick, so I was forced to resort to dicey hand picking the 'fraidy cat. It wouldn't be easy. I was up against twenty claws, the equivalent of twenty surgical slashers, and a mouthful of razor-sharp teeth. All part of the planet's number one Gladiator species. I assure you, it doesn't matter whether the cat you're up against is five hundred pounds or five. It's all dangerous.

Mama Cat had parked herself at the entry of her dark parlor. I did my best to coax her out, pleading my highly circumstantial case to spring her from her subterranean prison. Finally, Mama's empty stomach drew her out for dinner, and I scooped her featherweight into my hands. She was a silent black speck cowering in the depths of her cavernous container (a size 2 shoebox would have sufficed).

I'd been excited she had people, but then I learned that, when her people had been evicted, they'd moved on, leaving behind their furry family members to fend for themselves. I will spare you the expletives that, perhaps, fell from my mouth. Rest assured, they were colorful enough to put the "crazy" into "Cat Lady."

So she bunked in with our beasts. Little Mama lived in the shadows, hovering behind her merry kittens. Her tiny Tom had quickly shed his shy-guy shtick the second his little paws hit the high-pile good life, but she remained wary, her eyes always superglued to my every move.

Papa was assigned separate quarters. He, like all his deadbeat-dad brethren, steered clear of any actual paws-on parenting. But he was a good-looking cat, and his son was an equally devastating mirror image in miniature. We marketed them together as a dazzling boxed set, soon adopted and gone to greener pastures in a flash. Kitten number two was a natural-born enchantress in her own right. She sashayed up to the first critter shopper who came by, turned up her twelve-cylinder purr, and batted a come-hither blink, and just like that, she closed the deal. All it took was sixty seconds.

And poor Mama? She remained stewing in her corner, still a tangle of nerves. Tinkerbell had suffered from her abandonment, like all furry rejects from fair-weather families. Without a "Dear Fluffy" farewell note to howl over, Tinkerbell was caught in the precarious life-limbo between the only thing she knew—her past—and the scary world she now inhabited—us. We knew we'd need to piece together that shattered little soul, but it proved to be an epic jigsaw puzzle. Chips was with me; he always ended up on the tough-nut-to-crack committee, as we awaited the *I'm okay/You're okay* lightbulb moment in her little head.

We had to have patience. Any hiss-to-kiss change would be gradual, and on the cat's own terms. We'd learned, through long experience, that even certifiable basket cases just about always step up to the people-pleasing plate sooner or later.

With her offspring gone without so much as a backward glance at good ol' Mom (parenting is a heartbreaking business), we dove into her extreme makeover. We started by simply talking to her. We shared our own backstories (because nothing breeds bosom-buddy success like spilling secrets), we read insightful op-ed pieces out loud (so Tinkerbell would get used to our voices), we led by example (a sweet smooch from Chips's lips to my cheek), we played possum (not a muscle moving), but mostly we sat. And sat. And sat. And sat some more, slowly wooing the lonely kitty out of her shell.

Only to find a tyrant lurking beneath that wallflower façade! Once she had it, she would demand our undivided attention with all of her five pounds of determination (though a sneeze would still send her scurrying into the corner). Not exactly Pussycat Playmate of the Month material, but she had turned our way.

In all of this, Peter Pan was still around. We'd had high hopes for him, but the little critter had become paralyzed at every turn. He and Tinkerbell, both, scampered away from any alien being. Now usually I employ an effective divide-and-conquer strategy, but with these two, I merged them together. I had hoped for a meager boost if they each had a buddy. (Okay, what I had *really* hoped for was a sliver of my non-animal life back.) What I got instead was brilliance! Pairing up those two pet rejects proved positively transcendent. Tinkerbell had a protective streak a mile wide; without her own kittens there to hover over, she took a timid (and towering) Peter Pan under her small wing with mother-knows-best fervor. And in no time, she grew into her name, all stardust and moonbeams to match her pixie moods. Like all good cat duets, Tinkerbell and Peter Pan developed their own secret squawk talk (a jibber jabber sound somewhere between Happy Parrot and Pissed Hyena). They became inseparable, as two small snouts squeezed into one bowl or a pile of fuzzy black body parts jumbled together in slumber. As Tinkerbell grew more confident in her surroundings, her tiny stature was totally trumped by her strutting self-image, ruling their roost with Napoleonic gusto. Peter Pan, now a big mama's boy, fell in line, rarely dissenting from his drill sergeant. He was comically cowed by that bossy little bit of cat.

My goal was never to collect cats. My goal was always to *protect* cats. Once I rescued them, I wanted them adopted in a good home.

And by good, I meant my want-ad wish list for the perfect pet parents was the size of a novel.

And of course I was politely ruthless in my screening process. I always "requested" (such a nice word) prospective pet owners cough up a significant chunk of change, a donation the size of a spay-and-neuter bill for our Hurrah-for-Hiss-terectomies Fund. Yes, it was a sugarcoated shakedown, but that major cash outlay also happened to be my surefire forever-family filter. It ferreted out any lazy Saturday-afternoon wanderers or commit-a-phobe flakes that might otherwise have slipped past my seventy-seven questions or my "something's fishy" sniff test. Because, of course, a decade or two of respectable room and board for Fluffy wasn't free. No money, no kitty.

I always offered a 100 percent cat-back guarantee. No matter my third-degree grilling, or my dinner-and-a-month-of-movies dollar demands, I accepted the inevitability of a half-hearted critter-parent dropout every blue moon. This all added up to a sound night's sleep for me, their control-freak foster mommy, now blessedly free from nightmares of purr-balls heading back to the pound, or worse.

Tracking down *the* Dream Team for our little Orphan Alley-Annies could be tricky business, but I'd discovered a few effective recruiting commandments for finding Fluffy and Fido's forever family, all the while weeding out the worst tabby-tempted two-legged train wrecks:

- Little kitties don't mix well with the four-and-under kid crowd. Tots with nonstop hands and feet equal trouble. Cats are *not* trifling trinkets to be dispensed like Dearfoams slippers.

- Callers with lousy pet-parent track records go no further. If they've admitted that kittens keep going AWOL or that Rover chased one too many cars, then they do *not* get a replacement from me.
- My critters, my rules:
  - A cat belongs on a leash (ha, ha, ha! There are, in fact, very few kitties willing to submit to the humiliating conscription of a *walk*) *or* indoor cats only.
  - Dogs belong on a people-piloted leash—*not* tied up like laundry on a line. Or they need to be behind a fence on part-time potty patrol. But mostly, they need to be devoting themselves to their true calling: drooling all over their new beloved family.
- They must be spayed or neutered. A simple little snip-and-stitch subtraction saves a whole lotta loot. (I've learned the cold-hard-cash argument is the quickest way to a harebrain's heart.) Nip that nonstop fur factory in the ovarian bud before you're in over your head and wallet.
- Diplomatic dissuasion (or a just-plain "*Don't!*") against any future furry fiascos. Like, you know, abandoning your new best friend.

So even though, months later, Tinkerbell and Peter Pan were still super spooked by anyone *not* Chips or me, I felt compelled to venture forth on a quest to find them a new home. Together. There was no question the socially inept couple would need to stay with each other. Finding only one happily-ever-after home was the only option. Notwithstanding my strong sentimental bias toward a two-cat home anyway, I knew that splitting up Tinkerbell and Peter Pan would wreak major havoc with the tiny progress they'd made in social skills.

A car payment's worth of ads later, a lone A-list candidate came forth. They were gentlefolk, oozing with long-haul backbone for the bumpy road ahead. But I warned them. Usually, I would prescribe the soon-to-be-adopted kitties to two weeks of R&R in a chaos-and-kid-free area as a cure for relocating the scaredy-cats. But with Tinkerbell and Peter Pan, I upped the dose: infinite under-the-bed rest for our charm-school flunkies.

I admit to tears when the perplexed pair parted. But I also admit to hundreds of Hail Marys and relief for the minor miracle of finding a willing and able match. And, yes, I admit to a heaping helping of fretting about all those hair-raising unknowns awaiting our wide-eyed cats beyond their safe-and-cozy cubbyhole.

But truly, I didn't worry right away when I saw Tinkerbell and Peter Pan's people pop up on my caller ID. I didn't have any reason to immediately jump to any *cat*aclysmic conclusions. I always invited my new adopters to call anytime. The cats' new family was just calling.

To give up.

Their professed bottomless well of pussycat patience had run dry. That one-way ticket to the Promised Land turned out to be a round trip to pet purgatory and back. But the cats settled back into their old haunts, peevishly speed-squabbling like Ricky and Lucy one minute, piled in repose the next. I've no doubt the odd couple must have wondered why they'd been sent off on such an outlandish odyssey in the first place.

At this bleak point, one might presume a throwing-in of the tried-my-best towel, declaring those cohorts' baggage too burdensome for a life beyond our doorstep and then stirring them gently into our household hodgepodge. But The Pauly Pet Sanitarium was already filled to capacity, with Mildred's Odd Squad putting a six-cat strain on square footage, above and beyond our "official" cats. Such semantics of "officialdom" were necessary, if only to fog up the whopping Pauly pets-per-capita count (perhaps slightly over Mayberry's pesky code). Oh, and it was a buffer (though admittedly flimsy) against fuming spousal ballistic. ("But Chips, they're not *all* ours!")

I just couldn't let Tinkerbell and Peter Pan stay. With endless meowing recruits around every corner, any backlog or (God forbid) breakdown of our alley-into-lap-cats assembly line would be a mathematical—and matrimonial—disaster (Chips's recurring nightmare: being sucked into a bottomless black hole of high-maintenance fur). It could grow. If it were Tinkerbell and Peter Pan now, what would happen when the next unadoptable cats came along? I knew of a couple who had succumbed to just such a fate. They'd started sheltering homeless dogs, a Heinz 57 here, two terrier types there, and then, suddenly, they had pugs and Pekingese and poodles—and poop—everywhere. Into the triple digits! I cannot even imagine the off-the-Richter scale bark-a-thons. So no, I couldn't start down that slippery slope.

Besides, Chips likes to believe he cleverly wrestled some sort of moratorium out of me. He'd been trained to always anticipate the worst, after long years of tricky maneuvering around landmines and lairs (and watching his peaceful home quickly morph into a private petting zoo), so he wanted a hundred-year freeze on the Permanent Pauly pets. Naturally, my own buffed and polished recollection is somewhat different: It was a classic he-said-she-said toss-up. (Well, okay, technically, Mr. Total Recall might be on high ground here—I guess I just like to throw the poor guy a Yes-Dear-you're-absolutely-right! bone every now and then—good grief, since when is it a felony to tell a fuzzy little fib in the name of husbandly harmony?) Yes, I admit we had our share of tense tabby-tabulation standoffs along the way (marriage isn't for sissies), with hazy departure dates and murky membership tallies floating in a domestic DMZ between his prudence and my whole-hog herd-happy im*pet*uosity.

And so, I gave Tinkerbell and Peter Pan a pep talk about personal responsibility and the joys of an adventurous life, and reprinted my pussycats' personal ad (Two hopeless homebodies with issues seeking slavish submission, prefer night owls). In time, another masochistic clan stepped up to the plate, saying all the right things about undaunted courage and a burning desire to kiss goodbye the rest of that year's evenings and weekends in order to woo the reluctant recruits. And so, a second teary adios to my mucho-miffed amigos, four panic-stricken eyes giving me *not-again?* glares on their way out the door. I couldn't take a deep breath during those incubating weeks.

Then, the dreaded dead-end voicemail: "No luck with the kitties . . . very, very sorry . . . blah, blah, blah." The poor mixed-up munchkins were probably starting to suspect that revolving door of field trips and turnarounds to be standard operating procedure in their weird new musical-people world.

They picked up right where they'd left off in our now-not-so-bad back bedroom, apparently bearing no ill will toward us for those two strange sabbaticals.

When the first speck of faith in my fellow humans kicked in again, I resumed what was beginning to look like Mission Impossible. With so many *pick-ME-pick-ME!* people pleasers filling shelters to the brim (far outnumbering their domestic prospects), I was clearly searching for a solid gold needle in the humanitarian haystack to take on such a labor of love.

That WANTED manuscript—uh, ad—netted an admirable sprinkling of iron-spined inquirers who put up with my hour-long Q and A. Lo and behold, one more promising prospect passed muster. Third time's the charm? I lowered our rootless pair into their plastic kitty caboose once more (Crazy Cat Lady Tip #27: Trying to railroad a Terrible Traveler into her roving prison cell is a guaranteed losing proposition. You might as well be pushing a greased pig with a mean pedicure. Instead, turn that instant-nightmare-maker on its side and let gravity get your slippery character into her meow-mobile.) I crossed every last finger and toe.

When a few nerve-racking weeks trickled into months of white-flag-free optimism, I allowed myself to nibble on the possibility of fait *finally* accompli! But then I learned that Peter Pan and Tinkerbell had indeed inched their way out of their subterranean seclusion, and then there was eggshell walking around the skittish cats, so not long after, the new husband ordered the removal of the cats posthaste.

I approached Chips with a super-sweet *What do you think, honey?* How could we *not* now keep these two creatures, after three disastrous tries? Hadn't the involuntary vagabonds racked up enough turmoil and travel miles for two lifetimes?

Chips didn't even balk.

When Tinkerbell and Peter Pan returned, they returned to Neverland, a home-sweet-home terra firma they would never have to leave. It's true they were never officially promoted beyond green-card status. The chronic probationers loosely wove themselves into our warehouse of misfits. Peter Pan still struggled with herd-nerd self-esteem, pussyfooting around the perimeter of the pack, and Tinkerbell hung on to every last hissy-fit bit of her little-cat complex. Age and assimilation sapped some of the amplitude from their strange screech-owl chatter and loosened Tinkerbell's snug apron strings from around her great big mama's boy, but faced with any hint of peril, they still hightailed it to that sub-Serta bunker, melting into an anonymous black mound of scaredy-cat courage.

But in the end, they lived happily ever after.

Chapter 7

Once recent Christmas I was at the mall, waiting for my husband. I had ended up stationing myself on the railing above Santa's Workshop, where the big man himself was taking pictures with kid after kid after kid. My own girls are grown; Santa visits were long in the past. But I was entranced as a voyeur of the families. One mom, with two children, an older daughter and younger son, did the familiar parent-shuffle, trying to get both kids comfortable on Santa's lap. The kids weren't crying. In fact, the little boy, maybe five, was squirming with too much excitement. He had on a wide smile but had no interest in flashing it for the camera. The girl, maybe seven, looked as exasperated as her mom, clearly annoyed her brother was ruining her moment.

I smiled myself—and then surprised myself. I'd assumed I'd have started strolling down memory lane, reminiscing over my own daughters' Santa visits in this very mall, but instead, I thought about the family. I wondered where in the city they were from. I wondered what brought them to the mall on that specific day, at that specific moment. Had they planned the visit for weeks? Had the mom swerved the car into the parking lot at the last minute? So many assumptions; maybe they weren't from here. Maybe they were visiting. Maybe they didn't have a car. Maybe the mom wasn't the mom or the kids weren't siblings. But it didn't matter; the moment, and all the stories I spun up about them, reminded me of a once-favorite habit that had died off in recent years: people-watching.

The pandemic was one reason; there *were* no mall Santas, let alone malls in which to watch others. No one on the street, in cafés, or elsewhere. And when lockdown restrictions eased, I had shifted careers. I was no longer teaching in a classroom; I was writing, editing, and book coaching full time. My home was my office, my office my home, and rarely did I need to venture out.

I'd forgotten how much I loved to spin those very stories, fantasies, as much as my imaginings about joining Betsy at her practically perfect pal Sally's house, so I took in the crowd at the mall. The bustle and hurry of people in and out of stores, the squeak of a stroller passing by, the half-sentences I overheard, like a Doppler effect, zinging louder the closer they got, then fading before I could hear their whole conversation.

I think we need to get . . .

Get what? I wanted to know.

No, that's not right, it's . . .

What? What isn't right?

. . . if we just try . . .

Try what?

I'd never know, of course, but simply being around this festive mass of humanity reminded me of something I hadn't realized I'd dismissed: simple human connection.

I found myself musing about others, too, now that my imagination had been set free. The car that zipped by me on the highway, where was the driver going so fast? Why did the white van turn into the donut shop? What was the driver getting? Where were all these cars going? What lives were they returning to—or running from? The dog walkers strolling by my window, some of whom I recognized, some of whom I didn't, what were they leaving behind as they leashed their dogs? A crying kid? An angry spouse? A silent house?

It wasn't until I read a familiar name on the news that I became aware of my hobby's limitations: I had been concentrating my observations on only people I had physically seen. With more than eight billion people on the planet, I was working from a very small pool. But then I read an article about a woman with the same last name as my husband's. Since it was a less-common spelling of the name and my husband comes from a huge extended family that I most definitely cannot keep track of, it caught my eye. Though she lived on the other side of the country, was this person a relative? It turns out, no, she wasn't, but I turned my imagination to her life. If we weren't her relatives, who were? And had she always lived on the West Coast, or was she a recent resident? From there, my people-"watching" world expanded. I work with clients all over the world; I've often thought of them and their lives, but that's not the same thing because I can talk to them, learn about them, *befriend* them. But it did get me thinking about *their* neighbors and friends, and the people *they* might see at the mall. The world is random, but is it? Years ago, when my husband and I lived in Tanzania for a summer, we met an Australian and a Brit. They were strangers to each other—only, the Australian's roommate was friends with the Brit's cousin. And we made this discovery in the middle of Africa!

I began thinking more about how we can be connected. Not how we *are* connected (eight billion people and all . . .) but how many people *I* know who know others, who know others, who know others. The game of Six Degrees of Kevin Bacon, in which the theory posits that each and every one of us is connected to everyone else by only six degrees of separation. (I can attest to this; I am two people removed from Prince Harry because I had the supreme privilege of meeting his mother, Princess Diana, in person when I was a kid!)

Connections.

Yet Betsy didn't fit.

Yes, I'd met her husband, but that was after she died, and there was no person who knew her who knew someone else who knew someone else who knew me. I had "met" Betsy because her husband chose to reach out to a professional writer and editor. That's it.

A good friend of mine from my university days had gone on to write his own memoir. I reveled in his story because I recognized some shared moments. *Oh wow, he's writing about* that *time!* I felt connected to him because of our once-shared experiences, and felt privileged as I was reading it. *I* was one of a handful of people who'd known him then.

Shockingly, that's exactly how I felt when I began reading Betsy's animal tales.

I felt *privileged*, like I knew her.

I felt like I'd always known her, that I was *already* closer to her than the family I spotted with Santa, or the not-relative across the country, or even Prince Harry.

And I thoroughly enjoyed his memoir.

So why, with my self-proclaimed two-degree separation from royalty, did I better identify with Betsy over the heartfelt, honest, and authentic memoir of a prince?

Because, for all Prince Harry's openness, I also knew the final product I held in my hand was polished and shined for public consumption.

The Betsy in front of me, with only a draft of her stories on the page, was raw vigor. She had planned to revise and edit; she wasn't a fool about the writing process, but she'd never had the chance. So I saw before me her first brain dump, the purest, messiest, not-always-comprehensible, most honest (and some would argue the hardest) part of that writing process. It took time to parse through her language and structure and meaning, but it was rewarding in a way I could never have appreciated from my living writers with whom I work. Because *this* was all I had.

To understand Betsy was to understand her words. To understand her words was to understand Betsy.

Connection.

Marvelous Marvin

It's true that while I was widely recognized as a fully tenured, foaming-at-the-mouth Crazy Cat Lady, my day job was actually Starving Artist. Well, starving only for sales, admittedly. I acknowledge making art is only remotely approaching actual *work,* often dissed for its minimum paycheck and maximum fun factor. And yes, to fun, but also yes, to making some money. After all, it was the boomtown 1980s that bankrolled Dallas's most notorious habit of shop-till-you-drop conspicuous consumption of any shiny new thing not nailed down.

And then *poof!* Us poor, fur-brained Paulys fell right off the end of the earth, beyond the last outlying crop of mushrooming McMansions, into the deep, dark abyss of molded Jell-O salads, Knights of Pythias pancake feeds, and head-to-toe Walmart wardrobes.

My very own Mayberry. I was sanctimoniously resigned to the complete cultural kibosh that six hours beyond Porsches and Perrier would ensure. No doubt my meager-moneyed expressive enterprise would fade in favor of cute crocheted toilet-paper toppers and polka-dot plywood backsides gracing every turnip plot.

Well, wonder of wonders, I had to humbly eat crow. Civilization as we knew it did not liquefy like the Wicked Witch at the onset of Dorothy's bucket. We may have been leaving oil-slicked Oz, but we arrived in a land of beautiful aesthetic commerce of which Getty and Guggenheim would have been proud.

Among the artistic crowd was my Mayberry framer, a major flake whose talent nonetheless overrode his cannabis-laden incoherence and consequent state of chronic delays. Chips and I had been visiting, an eleventh-hour retrieval of my latest batch of two-by-three-feet pictures, but still we had to wait while my hippy-dippy art carpenter blearily applied the finishing touches. Happy Hour was in full swing next door at Marvin's Highball, and we watched with bemused curiosity as a tawdry mix of smoke, neon, and beer-fueled commotion spilled out onto our sidewalk.

Suddenly, a dark shadow came to life, a sorry scarecrow of a dog (who was still the size of a wolf) pacing near the pub's door. Naturally, I could not sit still. I pushed off my truck and meandered into Marvin's to search for a doggy daddy or mutt mommy. But among the well-oiled patrons, none claimed the poor pup.

Obviously, we could not leave our forlorn find to the mean streets of this ramshackle zip code. His prospects of surviving, let alone thriving, were dismal. Clearly we needed to make room in our sardine-packed pickup for yet another down-and-out candidate.

Chips, my ever-clever Mr. Fix-It, scavenged one of his ancient neckties from a bag destined, at least a good decade or so ago, to Goodwill. He fashioned a retro-chic restraint for the rail-thin hobo. The oh-so-'70s psychedelic silk bestowed a surprising touch of *GQ* distinction to the *before* beast, foreshadowing all the brighter days of the soon-to-be debonair Mr. *After*.

Our truck cab transported an improbable amalgamation of cargo that evening: nicely trimmed art, an unruly tramp in formal attire, and two bedraggled night owls making their appointed rounds in cozy chaos.

As Chips had been co-conspirator in that curbside rescue, he took charge of the christening: Marvelous Marvin. I approved. It captured our new friend's serious uptown swag in spite of his not-so-dreamy downtown drag.

En route to debonair-hood, Marvelous Marvin returned from a deluxe snout-to-stern pampering at Salon du Veterinarian, and we did indeed marvel at the handsome devil now before us. The full-service doggy day spa had discreetly removed any further thoughts of fatherhood from Marvin's future with their "snip, sew, and go" service, but it did nothing to tame the wild within. By bedtime, Marvin was bouncing off the walls and devouring furniture at an alarming rate. (Evidence Exhibit A: an "interpretively carved" remains of a game table whose chew-toy chairs had to be put out of their Marvin-induced misery. It was ambitious work for a single afternoon home alone.) He also took to expelling digestive byproducts at whim, which warranted a den to call his own as a way to nip those messy mishaps in the bud. Any rookie woofer great and small knows there is no bathrooming in their own bedroom. But how to find a cage big enough for our wildebeest wannabe? Our own inventory of critter containers had nothing nearly large enough to accommodate our heifer-sized hound. The search was on.

Finally, I found a crate (the size of a studio apartment) in the local farm store. Its original purpose was a moving van for a toddler cow. Huh. Who knew such items even existed? But exist they did, and cavernous it was. I was even able to navigate it quite nicely without spinal injury during my DIY demos for Marvin, the reluctant tenant. But in spite of its palatial square footage and cushy man-cave decor, the crate was not a right-away winner. Corralling Teflon Marvin into it was as effective as corralling a congenial greased board. The task demanded steady wits and mouthwatering morsels tossed into the back of it before we could slam the crate door shut with all the bullfighting bravado we could muster. Marvin, Eveready Energizer Bunny that he was, never voluntarily checked himself in, but once all the prison-pandemonium simmered, Marvin momentarily mellowed. He would take a Milk-Bone break to recharge those high-voltage batteries, no doubt daydreaming of doggy parole from the crate-jail.

We had a job ahead of us. It took up hefty chunks of daylight to refine Mountain-Man Marvin into something closer to family-flavored pet. His trick of pretending he was a sixty-pound torpedo just wasn't going to cut it if a desperate-for-a-dog family showed up to test-drive our lead-pawed Marvio Andretti. He was a leaping, lunching linebacker of an animal; to train him (without ripping off my rotator cuff), we needed space.

Chips, he of two hundred pounds of marshmallow mush, took the lead. Rather, the softie would often let the critters lead. Normally, Chips would allow our own dog, Daisy Mae, to wander whimsically on their midnight treks, following her insatiable snout wheresoever it might take them, racing, then quick-sniff stopping in backyards and begonia beds. So Chips resolved to do the same with Marvin, allowing him geographic carte blanche on their nightcap outings. Marvin was thrilled after his dull days of my own plow-horse prodding during our walks. With Chips, it was always more man-on-leash than dog-on-leash, with four long legs and two slightly longer legs streaking through our sleeping town. Two feet pounded in punishing overdrive, just barely pacing four frolicking paws trotting along. Chips, though at his pinnacle of buff-and-tough Iron Man mojo, would often hobble home sweat-soaked and panting like a dog himself while Iditarod-ready Marvin, neither wet nor winded, reveled in that Rocket Man warm-up tempo.

One such heart-healthy evening in November, Chips and Marvin, my very own dog-driven Daytona team, detoured cross-country. On this night, they raced through the wooded campus of a Vietnamese Catholic monastery, which had been expansively set up with Christmas lights and large nativity scenes. The official "plug-in" for the gorgeous scenes had not yet happened, thus the displays were all camouflaged by nightfall.

Zing!

A sharp wire struck Chips as Marvin roared ahead, right into a display. The wooden boards were knocked off their guidewire moorings, and in a dominos of biblical proportion, down tumbled David the Giant Slayer and all his other beefed-up biblical cohorts. Chips and Marvin stood, stunned, as they listened to the carnage of clanging and crashing wreckage.

Thankfully, they were both unharmed, though we could not say the same about David and/or Goliath. Chips made a mea culpa call, and before long, the scenes had been restored and the Old Testament team twinkled brightly on opening night alongside the rest of their brilliant brigade.

As for Marvin, he soon learned to tamp his energy. When we polished his rough edge to a perfect "good-boy!" glow, we unearthed our natural-born Mr. Nice Guy. Another novella of an ad later, and we connected with a perfect prospect—within shouting distance at that! The congenitally cheerful Metcalfs, who were both community pillars and personal pals, came to meet our equally effervescent Marvin. It didn't always happen, God knows, but this match was a meant-to-be Dream Team, one I yearn for for all our barking benchwarmers. Marvin and the beaming squad of sons all wrestled like littermates, and despite prudent, let's-sleep-on-it determination from Mother

Metcalf (giving her the illusion of objective decision-making when, in reality, love-at-first-woof had long since won out), by morning, the merry Metcalfs had one more mischievous male barking away at their breakfast table. From lean, lonely beginnings to a bottomless biscuit bowl and built-in band of brothers (not to mention summers in the Rockies and a sofa all his own), Marvelous Marvin Metcalf had finally reached the top of his K9-karma ladder.

"Oh my God, Marvin!" Chips laughed when I asked for more detail about his misadventures with Christmas scenery. Betsy's story was charming. I laughed as I read about it, but of course, Betsy was recounting the events secondhand; unlike Betsy herself, for this one small portion of this one story, I had access to the protagonist himself.

"The Christmas displays were beautiful," Chips reminisced. "The property of the monastery, which had been an old college campus, was large, with roads crisscrossing it. Every year, they would put on a display that people could drive through. Some of the displays, the size of billboards, would be a story, like Jonah and the Whale. Here's Jonah, and there's a whale, and the lighting would move so it looks like Jonah ends up in the mouth of the whale. Yes, David was there, too. One of the rocks glows across the sky and hits Goliath, who then falls down. It wasn't only Goliath who fell down that night!

"On that walk, I'd told Marvin, 'You just run as fast as you can as long as you want to.' I took off the leash and we took off. I had run maybe twenty yards when I felt something slap across my chest. I didn't understand what it was at first, but it was powerful enough to make me stop. It turns out there were guidewires holding up the billboards. One of them had snapped, and the billboard starts to tip over, hitting the next and the next like dominos. ***Bang, bang, bang!*** 'Marvin!' I called. 'We're going home!'

"I called up the monastery at, like, 10:30 p.m. 'There's been a little incident with your David and Goliath,' I admitted. 'A wire broke and the whole thing collapsed and if you have any questions, my name is Steve Smith,' and then I hung up! Now, Steve Smith was a good friend of mine and a big deal in our community."

I laughed as much hearing Chips's account as reading about Betsy's. "Did Steve get in trouble?"

Chips chuckled. "Nah, they simply propped it all back up."

"And Marvin? He had a happy ending, too?"

Chips smiled. "That match worked out beautifully."

Chips plays a supportive role throughout Betsy's stories, and, as Chips himself would acknowledge, that was his own role in Betsy's life as an animal-welfare advocate, too.

"It meant so much to her to have the animals that my reaction was, we'll do whatever it takes to address it. I never said we've got eight cats, so we can't take any more on. It wasn't going to happen. If there was an animal in need, that took priority. If it was that important to her, it was that important to me."

If it was that important to her, it was that important to me.

In her stories, Betsy is good-natured about any small spats she and Chips might have had about her dedication to her strays, but always Chips is her hero.

The love and respect between them is undeniable, crystal clear in the stories written before Betsy died and abundantly heartfelt in the chats with Chips after.

It was *their* connection that, too, drew me into Betsy's universe. It was where I appreciated not only Betsy's authenticity, something I greatly admired, but also how much having *support* for that authenticity matters. Betsy could be her true, full, real, complete, passionate, heated, dedicated, crazy-cat-lady self because she had a husband who loved Betsy's true, full, real, complete, passionate, heated, dedicated, crazy-cat-lady self.

Connection.

It comes in the form of imaginary musings about strangers on Santa's knee or kinships with people whose names are shared even if they aren't related. They are the spiderwebs, the gossamer threads, the silver streaks that bind us all, from a home in Ottawa to a storybook world in Betsy's own Mayberry of Carthage, Missouri.

But what allows us to put ourselves out there, what gives us the courage to reach out, to say, *Hey, this is me!*, to write, like my university friend, or Prince Harry, or, yes, Betsy in her stories about cats and dogs, is the connection with those who already love us. Connection is both the single string and also the tensile strength that binds us together as our true, authentic selves.

And I got that all from a dog named Marvin.

Chapter 8

The sense of pandemic isolation snuck up on me very, very gradually. I was like the proverbial boiled frog, unaware that the pot of water in which I floated was getting hotter and hotter and hotter until it was too late. Instead, my pandemic experience started out with, of all things, a very in-person, very frenetic, very busy night of parent-teacher interviews. Isolation seemed, in that moment, both a fantasy and a state to which one could only aspire.

At 3:00 p.m. on Thursday, March 12, 2020, just two days before the start of our March break, the Ontario government announced that schools would be closed for the two weeks following the break. The announcement also assured parents that teachers would provide meaningful work.

At 3:30 p.m., my endless hours of parent meetings began. Hundreds of parents roamed the school halls to meet with the hundred or so teachers, and on each of their minds was no longer the question of how their child was doing in class but ***What meaningful work will you provide?*** Oh my god! As if I knew! We'd not yet had direction from our principal, nor the board, but then, how could we have, with only half an hour's notice?

None of us were ignorant of Covid at that time. It had been in the news but always something that happened at a distance. "It's in China," I reassured my then-early-teen daughter. When the first Canadian case was reported, I reassured her. "It's in B.C., a long way from us." So when the Ontario government announced school closures, the impacts remained abstract. That night, none of us wore masks, and there was no such thing as social or physical distancing—in fact, there were still handshakes. Many of us laughed at what we initially thought was an overreaction. We didn't claim to be the experts; we were willing to defer, but really, closing the schools for a total of three weeks? Was that necessary?

I went into school the next day, Friday, March 13, 2020. As usual, I wrote the date on the blackboard. I had no idea that not only would I not see the inside of that classroom for more than six months but that that would also be the very last day I'd ever teach a normal class in a normal classroom in person. By the time all the restrictions had lifted in Ontario, I had moved on from the education system.

Not much course content got taught that day, to be sure. Everyone was buzzing about the World Health Organization's declaration of a pandemic. What did that mean? What would happen next? Not just my questions but most of my students', too. I had no answers. No one did.

As the world shut down, my own world did not quiet. In fact, it gained screeching urgency because, soon, I was expected to teach online. Virtually. I was freaking. I was an old-school teacher. I *wrote* on my blackboard. With *chalk*! Technology wasn't unwelcome in my classroom, it was just unnecessary. We had books, and we had paper, and unless accommodations were warranted, we had everything we needed.

Teaching online to students who did not sign up for online was a nightmare. Students, understandably, did not have to turn their cameras on during our live "classes." I was teaching into a black hole.

This might have been a premonition of my coming isolation, but my life was a flurry of online activity. We were meeting constantly as a staff, trying to learn new technology; I was in constant contact with worried parents; and, oh yeah, my own family was now home full-time. My two daughters had their own online school, and my husband, a federal public servant, was now locked away in our home office. Isolation? Hah!

As news stories kept coming, warning people about the effects of isolation and lack of connection with friends and family, I scoffed. Not at the reality for other people, but that *I* would ever be affected. I appreciated how hard it must be for people who lived alone, or who rarely saw others. I was fine.

But as the months passed, as the restrictions eased and then returned, and then eased again, as my own friends fell away, as my work-a-day banter with colleagues disappeared, I began to wonder. Was there something to this isolation business after all? Slowly, eventually, as the world almost-sort-of righted, I began to feel the low-grade crush of it all. By this time, my kids had returned to modified versions of in-person school, and my husband, too, had returned to the office. And by this time, too, I'd switched careers, the right move for me, but now my whole business was virtual.

In other words, I was now alone all day every day.

Just as people could again spread their wings, I found myself drawing inward.

No surprise I turned to books. Obviously there's no original insight in recognizing that we can feel connected through the written word, but original or not, it was nonetheless true. The more I retreated, the more I read. The more I read, the less I felt the need to retreat.

Still, social isolation was real, even if my experience had been delayed. What I had once known, the familiar rhythm of family and friends, never returned to what it had been before the pandemic, and it took me a while to adapt. I had been a reluctant user of videoconferencing—I was all about *in-person* connections—but the more virtual meeting I had with clients and fellow authors, the more they turned into much-needed social visits. I got to know people I'd never met. And it was astounding what I learned (something millions had discovered long before me)—that connections don't have to be physical. Again, no original insight, but what it did do was open my eyes to a wider world of possibilities. I could nurture these burgeoning relationships online. Through texts or emails, or video chats, I could make new friends without being in the same city, country, or continent. And by new friends, I actually mean real friends, not social media "friends." Like the people I'd once turned to in person, I'd found a community online. I finally understood that these virtual connections were as valuable and powerful as any friendships I'd developed before.

So if I could expand my once-limited perspective of connection to the virtual world, it wasn't, in fact, much of a stretch to find connection not just in literature with fictional characters but with the authors themselves.

Even if they'd already died.

Two Furry Flashbacks

When we arrived in Mayberry, we were but two small-town tenderfoots, searching for our very own Green Acres. Yet we were stymied, then stalled, in our hunt for our Hollywood-set homestead. The culprit was our long list of picky prerequisites—and a (very) short list of potential properties. We lusted for something huge and historic, and so we put out a wide broadcast for help. We didn't get it. Instead, we got local horse traders drooling over city-slicker dollar signs peddling old teardowns at jackpot prices. No thank you.

Fine, we thought, *we'll park ourselves somewhere temporarily. We'll find a halfway-habitable stopgap house in the meantime.* Only, with our (growing) petting zoo in tow, we had as much difficulty with halfway okay as we did with permanent dream home. Yet just as we were about to be hogtied into some leaning two-by-four trouble ahead of imminent homelessness, fate kindly punted us a perfect pied-à-terre. We had found a sweet little entr'acte house, set on the edge of Eden, wrapped in woods and water.

One dismal November afternoon, as I was navigating through the forest along a rain-slicked lane, an odd purse of color caught my eye. The last flaming riot of leaves had dropped; the now-topless canopy had exposed its interior in which I could see two rusty mounds lying side by side. I passed through a puddle to get to them, and the splash suddenly brought one of the pair to life. The other, an inanimate pot, kept deathly still. The one who could breathe was a scrawny scrap of a mutt, and I was immediately set with furry worry. I set down my bag of perishables (the ice cream already well on its way back to needing a straw instead of a spoon) and slowly moved forward. The dog slinked away. I took another step forward; he slinked back two.

I was angry. Without a doubt, he was victim of a classic dump-and-drive. He was hungry and tired, yes, but wary. He would not quickly or easily come to me.

So I raced home only to return with proper Fido-fishing provisions. When I arrived, he'd gone back to snuggling with the piece of scrap metal (any pot in a storm, I guess). Snow was forecast, and indeed, a few flakes had already dusted the bashful boy. The mercury was nose-diving. It was urgent I collect the mutt before nightfall.

I settled in as close as Jittery Junior would allow. I laid out the day's personalized game plan, starting with well-tossed treats, which the half-starved hobo swallowed whole. I waxed poetic about the benefits of central heating as we two entered a shivering state of frozen-frenemy empathy.

"Come on, buddy," I coaxed as each hypothermic half hour brought me slithering a bit closer. The gray daylight faded, receding into charcoal dust. "Come on, we gotta go . . ."

I leaned in to place the leash around his nervous neck. He balked and backpedaled out of reach. I groaned, but I had rabid resolve, so I recommenced my rear-end crawl, whispering all the right tender-toned thoughts. Somehow I either broke through his barbwire-barricaded heart or I just wore down the last of his dejected defenses, and he finally submitted to being scooped up, schlepped over rough ground, and juggled into the car without a peep of protest.

Once my orphans are safely in my arms, it's often the last time I'll think about their desperate days of old. Maybe it's cowardly, but I really don't see the point in trying to retrace their troubled trails. I have no meowing medium with whom I could consult, no barking crystal ball to browse the bad old days. Instead, I would just end up spitting four-letter nails at imaginary numbskulls, which hardly helps the tattered creatures at my feet. I've often wondered how (sainted) shelter workers can so often deal with not just the emotional toll of the endless river of furry refuse but also their don't-give-a-damn depositors who spout excuses and ooze irresponsibility. When I come across my strays, their horrible humans have long since disappeared. But while I don't have to discover any sanity-saving techniques to survive such encounters, I also don't have the capability of collecting backstories. I am limited only to the biographical tidbits at hand.

In this case, I knew only that the dog was unfed, unaltered, and uneducated. He was maybe an Irish setter. Or not. And he lacked the least little bit of *good-boy!* belief in himself. I was not surprised, then, that my usual all-points bulletin didn't turn up any human. I would have to find him a new BFF. After my usual fine-tooth-flea-comb and germs-to-worms once-over, he was ready.

One promising candidate came forward (even after my interrogation, cleverly disguised as coffee talk, of course). She requested to bring along Baby, her lonely, long-tailed princess sorely in need of a buddy. Her princess turned out to be a

150-pound baby brontosaurus of an English bullmastiff! This burly breed was best known for their original day job as yard guards, able to detain uninvited visitors in iron-trap gums or simply deposit their tonnage atop the drop-ins until directed by their owners to do otherwise. Talk about a Tom-and-Jerry mismatch—my little unmighty mouse sharing the Man Muncher's wading-pool bowl of kibbles?

Yet Baby's devoted owner vigorously defended her darling girl's docility. "How about a trial run?" she suggested.

To which I added multiasterisked conditions—the most important of which would be that any said meeting would take place on my home turf. Even then, all I could imagine was the dark dread of a rag-doll-limp little redhead dangling from barking bear jaws.

On the day of the visit, Baby's owners jumped out of their minibus, beaming with Christmas-in-July goosebumps, but where was Baby? They opened the rear hatch, and, my god, a huge bouncing blob of jiggling jowls came crashing out, hell-bent on covering me with waterfall-of-drool kisses.

Relieved by half (the happy-go-lucky heifer-sized dog clearly had no current interest in tearing me limb from limb), I held my breath, picturing my wimpy little mutt going nine rounds (ha, nine seconds!) with this galloping beast. The saddle-worthy dog lumbered through the yard like a Shetland pony while I fetched her unsuspecting love interest/lunch.

As I tiptoed out with my little mutt, Baby stampeded over and—much to my amusement—somersaulted into an Olympic-backstroke *Howdy!* That flashing-neon "Wanna-be-pals?!" was instantly answered with a belly-up *You-betcha!!* (A pretty neat trick, turning Underdog into Rin Tin Tin in five seconds flat.) All we could see was a whirlwind of helicopter tails and leaps cavorted off in a dog dance of complete joy.

Needless to say, I hugged my little orphan goodbye that day, fighting back the farewell-forever tears. The lovestruck groupie shared no such sweet parting sorrow, glued as he was to his great big bosom buddy's side. He even disappeared into the car without so much as a backward nice-to-know-ya glance. My momentary letdown—feeling like leftover chopped liver next to his new superhero—couldn't compete with that magical K9 Kodak moment of seeing my sad little Humpty Dumped-y's broken spirit brought back to the happiness every dog deserves.

Shifting down a few gears, Chips and I eased into the simple charms and sleepy pace of our Missouri Mayberry (the anti-Manhattan), a place blissfully devoid of rush hour and road rage (the closest thing to traffic trouble being friendly four-way logjams, Goober, Gomer, Barney, and Aunt Bea all waving . . . *Go right ahead! . . . Oh, hi, Fred! . . . You first!*), crime (locks lay idle and Chevy keys in the ignition), and chaos. The townsfolk had donuts and the daily dirt at ten. We city slickers, still adjusting, were just getting to our granola and the daily grind. Then they had a beefy blue-plate special at the stroke of noon—try, for us, a spirulina-green smoothie at two. And then they rolled up the abandoned sidewalks by seven (more like midnight taps for us Paulys). It was all a picture-perfect panorama of homespun happiness.

No surprise, you rack up a lot of free time with five-minute cross-town commutes and a somewhat skimpy cultural smorgasbord—calf roping, line dancing, and a leftover double feature at the Route 66 drive-in notwithstanding. My post-canvas-painting hours started to stretch out before me, and so, following in Rodney Dangerfield's illustrious ivory-tower footsteps, back to school I went, picking up right where I'd left off (dear Lord) a quarter century ago.

One fine day, I was crossing campus in pursuit of a senior citizen student ID when I caught sight of a paper-thin mama cat strategically marching her squadron of apprentice mousers—three little soldiers trailing in single file—toward the sanctuary of a kitty-sized drainpipe. My unwitting approach instantly scattered the powder-puff platoon. No surprise that these featherweight super-spooks were on rat patrol; they looked spare and lean, no doubt living off anything Mama could snag. I spied a fuzzy little face peeking out from his concrete lair, and then, *poof*, empty pipe.

I knew they would officially be expelled, their dead-end major in mooching and mousing coming to an end. It would call for a road trip to Lucky Cat College (a.k.a. University of Pauly). So, one by one, the slow-motion teacup kitties tiptoed into my all-you-can-eat buffet of a cage. With her shell-shocked brood safely under my halfway-to-housecat belt, Mama finally emerged, no doubt having witnessed their kit-napping. I saw her sniff the thin air into which her kittens had vanished, and then she bravely crept into that ravenous opening, like Alice through the looking glass, hoping to magically meet her lost little everythings on the other side. That heroic leap of motherly faith did indeed parachute her into a sweet reunion.

It got me thinking, yet again, of the root cause of my mission. Yes, I was saving strays, but why were there so many souls to save in the first place? Because of people who just couldn't seem to give a damn about spaying and neutering.

You see, Mama's single-parent predicament wasn't a matter of lackluster family values or willful wanton ways. She had simply answered an incessant Puss-in-Booty call. That celestial trigger works her entire sisterhood into a wild lather for whoopee quaintly called *heat*. In Mother Nature's foolproof fashion, she'd be hot to trot with every Tom, Dick, and Harry until firmly in the family way. A couple months later, her latest litter turns up, tenderly fed and fended for a couple more months, and then—*bam!*—Mama's right back at it with all the boys on the block, likely churning out two batches of juniors each and every sunny season of catly lust.

The mathematical trail of all that meowing monkey business is an avalanche of alley breeders. Its solution is to stop the tom-and-tabby snowball in its tracks. Just turn off that gushing spigot of sperm and spare critters with one small snip-and-stitch step for kitty, one giant away-with-strays leap for cat-kind. But you'd best put puss's nip-and-tuck on this week's to-do list. Like all exponential quantification, timing is everything. That one-handed critter counting suddenly catapults out of control like free beer at the frat house. Remember, $1 + 1 \times 8 + 8 \times 64 + 64 \times \ldots$ millions of surplus houseless mousers. And, since we humans do not go forth and multiply at anything remotely close to those computations, the pet-to-petter ratio quickly topples over. But reversing an equation can bring you right back to square one—one less kitty-mill mama and mass-production papa means a whole lot less purring pitter-patter. Hundreds less, thousands less, scrillions less lost little souls. And, now, hallelujah! All that pussycat

Planned Parenthood is finally taking hold. Gutter-guardian angels among us are crunching the astronomical furry numbers one quick trip to the vet at a time.

What's that you say? No hairball hanky-panky in *your* swanky alley? Come on, not noticing the Million Cat March right in front of your turned-up nose is quite an amazing optical delusion, because a cat's a cat. Tom is cut from the very same cloth as your in-house cat, *and* he and his alley harem proliferate at the very same preordained eye-popping rate as—and *with*—their brethren who are pets. Alley Sally actually has prize purrball potential—my biggest meowing mama's boys and good-as-gold girl mouse-scouts are all former growling gangbangers. Fixing every furry kitty saves a forest of tiny kittens from an extremely uncertain tomorrow. To those cold-blooded fatalists who'd declare the backstreet baby boom beyond all righting, I suggest we all start counting backward, fixing one chronic litter-bug after another until we find that purr-fect ratio of lap-minded applicants to "Welcome Kitty!" mats.

Our current college dropout's tummy tuck—as well as her latest little imps' impending impregnability appointments—would halt the output sure to follow. Kittens are ready for that piece-of-cake procedure from about four pounds up, so it's easy to get ahead of the must-mate game. After that groggy slumber party at the vet, they'll come home primed for a happy-go-lucky lap-hogging life without the Mt. Olympus of PMS or those tabby-craving tomcat troubles (we're talking all-night arias and competing pee sprees). And it's way better for her fortunate humans, too. They get to forgo the Furry-Girls-Gone-Wild dating game and maternity-ward high finances, not to mention finding forwarding addresses for bundle after bundle of joy.

But fixing Fluffy costs too much!

It's an argument I've heard again and again, so pardon my momentary soapbox to neuter some nitwit mythology about the fuzzball birds and bees. The one-time fee (less than a tightwad's night on the town) is a whole lot cheaper than forking out for kitty litter and cat food. And with programs and services out there for cash-strapped pet people, from Mayberry to Manhattan, empty pockets are no excuse.

Miss Mittens should manufacture a litter or two first, to mellow her out.

Utter hogwash! Maturity (not motherhood) will calm your curtain-climbing little friend. (Would feeding and fussing over a passel of greedy eating machines 24-7 soothe *your* nerves?) And getting rid of the estrogen-powered equipment means good riddance to all those hormonal hissy fits!

I want my little Bobby and Suzy to witness Mother Nature's placenta-packed pièce de résistance.

Madame Overactive Ovaries prefers privacy for the big event. (Who can blame her?) You can google a buffet of furry birds-and-bees-and-babies filmmaking on YouTube without all that mewling detritus.

If I fix Fido, he'll quit his guard-dog gig.

Fiddlesticks. All that over-my-dead-body watchkeeping radiates from his pack-man heart, not his one-track nuts. And, as he'll no longer be thinking with his below-the-belt brain, he'll hang around the house instead of chasing tail all over town.

Only the hairy little lady needs the knife. After all, Mrs. Minxy is the kitty incubator.

Duh. It takes two to tango. One locked-and-loaded dude can create a junkyard of juniors from his little black book of neighborhood nymphomaniacs.

Sex is really *important to me and I don't want to deprive my BFF of that hound-dog hokey-pokey.*

Oh, please! Don't confuse your selective gratification with your best barking buddy's. Red-blooded Rover won't notice any change in the moving-parts program or pine for the good old love-'em-and-leave-'em days.

Fixing Fifi L'Amour will make her fat and lazy.

Really, now, it's not exactly rocket science that too much munching plus too little locomotion equals balloon pets (and people). If your Romeo-no-more is rounding out beyond pleasingly plump, hoist the both of you off that Doritos-decorated couch and take a hike.

So, of course we made sure Mama and her college kitties were taken care of. And it wasn't easy, but we still *did* it.

Usually, with a snack and a few laps of snooping around their cushy new digs, most of our recently drafted rookies pick up some inkling of good domestic behavior. Not so with College Mama. If she was in an out-of-control frenzy in her cat-catching cage, she went into overdrive in her new twelve-by-twelve room, like some crazed Stephen King goblin emitting eerie spook-house moans and hair-raising promises of a shredding if I stepped one inch closer.

I was spellbound at her Superman (Supercat?) strength, flying up tall walls in a manic vertical rocketry. As she got used to her guest-bedroom bearings, retreat seemed the kindest (and safest) thing to allow the crazed Olympian a break from her heart-attack-bound high-jumping. As there appeared to be zero chance that the mad-as-hell mouser had ever savored a taste of the sweet life, I skipped all my pointless pavement pounding in search her nonexistent house number. Instead, I proceeded directly to the epic taming of the tortoiseshell shrew.

Food is darn good getting-to-know-you glue, particularly when poor puss has put up with an Old Mother Hubbard cupboard all her born days. But Mama, rechristened Mrs. Chippy, didn't seem interested in connecting her kibble to the well-doings of the Crazy Cat Lady. No matter how close I tried to get to her, my offerings didn't spark the usual kumbaya campfire singalong. Her "progress" was excruciatingly microscopic, evidenced only slightly by the slackening of wallpaper shredding. Now she would only shoot herself halfway up to the crown molding upon my entrance. I still encountered muffled mountain lion growls and burn-inducing glares thrown my way.

It took a long time before I could get my demonically possessed protégé checked in for her no-more-Mother's Day spay-spa pampering (under serious and steady sedation, needless to say). Her powder-puff gang meekly submitted to the same, all pip-squeak bravado melting into popeyed scaredy-cat soup at that brand-new brand of tabby terror.

Always the effort is worth it.

As the three kittens sprouted like furry beans, two of the tikes proved to be social Silly Putty and the third's spitfire threats waned into harmless exhales. Already they were undisputed itty-bitty-kitty heart melters, *the* hot ticket in the pet market. It was high time to book my superstars permanent gigs.

The two litter leaders, clowns that they were, easily marched into four lovestruck little arms, but my leftover runt we named Tiger Lily was still suspicious of me. Though I was the lunch lady, she would often flee in a freaked-out frenzy. Her antipathy toward us giant humans matched her mama's severe people allergies. The odds that either of those basket cases would warm our laps anytime soon was somewhere between bigfoot on *Dancing with the Stars* and yours truly devouring a veal chop. I tried, oh, I tried, but eventually, I had to admit I was full-on stymied by their remedial-charm-school stagnation. So I broke my own divide-and-conquer strategy *again*. (Like I usually broke every other fuzzy fuzzball rule written provisionally in kitty litter.) I reunited the intransigent twosome. And what happiness for Mama and her mini-me! Immediately, they settled into a sweetheart sandwich. With that victory, I had a shot. *Very* slowly, like snail's-pace slowly, I won them over, even if we had to concede to their evasion tactics. Only a very few eagle-eyed snoops had ever spotted the undercover chameleons (any unknown vocal cords sent them scurrying for deepest, darkest *gone*). The fascinating endeavors of their entwined souls made for some pretty *his*sterical Hairy Houdini disappearing acts for Chips and me, their only (and always amused) audience.

Mrs. Chippy and Tiger Lily also cemented proof of my long-held theory of the ironclad correlation between a puss's fur color and her particular personality. If you take our good old orange tabbies, the top of the lap-hogging food chain, you'll notice they are the fat-cat world's jovial used-car salespeople, head-of-the-line hedonists, and always willing to turn the other cheeky cheek. Their gadabout gray cousins are a close Miss (No-Hiss) Congeniality runner-up. They are unapologetic party animals, always on the prowl for good times and grub. Both are garden-variety every-cats, quintessentially memorialized by celebrity, commercial-crushing huckster Morris, that loveable lazybones on TV who quickly morphs into his meow-hound alter ego at the dinner bell.

But cats like Mrs. Chippy and Tiger Lily, the tortoiseshells, those Jackson Pollock-splattered kin to Picasso-cubed calicos, are the unvarnished vacillators and professional-grade second-guessers. They can be *purr*fectly nice part-time pals, but they can also perplex the unsuspecting and frustrate those pet owners in need of crowd control (you law-and-order lovers might want to take a hard left into Dogville). Clearly, they are Catdom's most camera-shy members. In their understated neutrals, they can easily vanish into the woodwork in a scary-fast second. Yet wherever our own two camo-coated scaredy-cats hid, they would still curl around and atop each other in every conceivable yin-yang position, melding into a blurred and purring background bliss. When I did finally find them, all snug together, my heart would always melt.

Is there any wonder this is my mission?

And here, after reading this story, is where I punched out a gleeful laugh. *Here*, I thought, *here is* my *people.* Betsy is my people. This woman whom I'll never have a chance to meet, whose life comes to me only through her prose, is a woman

I can get on board with. She had a heart of gold I admire, a willful personality I appreciate, and—most importantly—a sharp tongue, about which I am, and continue to be, unduly jealous.

I love Betsy's gentle humor, poking fun at herself and her wayward strays, her lighthearted, warmhearted tone, but I *love* Betsy's barbs. I am all for civil conversations, respect, tolerance, and understanding as we interact with each other. I am empathetic; I try hard to see where people are coming from, how and why they behave the way they do, but truthfully, it can be exhausting, and, yes, sometimes I just want to tear a strip off someone. *You did* what*? How* could *you? You moronic piece of sh—* You get the idea. Chips assures me Betsy was pleasant and contained in her criticism with people face-to-face, but I love that she felt free enough to say what she meant about *stupid people*. You don't want to spay or neuter your pet? Then, yeah, you're a nitwit. You think it's fine to dump your feline? Then you're an ass. Oh, and here's why. Betsy wasn't afraid to let loose in her cutting tone. Admittedly, I was reading a draft; would Betsy have toned down her rhetoric in revisions? Possibly. Maybe. Or not. But that's why I loved reading her rough copy. I was getting Betsy unvarnished. I'm not suggesting we do away with revisions or editors when we write (no one would be able to read let alone decode my first-draft ramblings of my own writing!), but it gave me a unique insight into a woman who no longer had a literal voice.

We have a bad habit in our society of dampening women's passions. Anger or frustration, no matter how valid, are held against us. We are labeled *hiss*terical. We are labeled Crazy Cat Ladies.

Betsy owned her anger. She didn't apologize for her passions.

She was a straight shooter.

Yeah, my kind of people.

Chapter 9

Some of my favorite stories are about women "villains." You know, the mythical female characters described as evil, dark, ruthless, and devious, who will stop at nothing to get their own way, corrupting our valiant (male) heroes along the way—characters like the Greek goddess Circe, the Israeli queen Jezebel, or the Disney villain Maleficent. Each of these women has a "reputation," and given what we know from the "original" stories, they should be shunned, cast out, set aside, and vanquished before their evil ways can infiltrate and infect the good among us. Yet as we all know, history (and myth and legend and mid-century movies) are written by the victors, which, in these cases (as in all cases when discussing the passions of women) are men. Stories are framed according to their own prejudices and biases, and, if I may overgeneralize, men don't often take kindly to strong, passionate women. But when you take the Circes and the Jezebels and the Maleficents of the world and you tell *their* stories from *their* perspectives, as many successful authors and filmmakers have done, we can see not just that their actions might have been justified but that their actions weren't, in fact, evil at all. These women were strong, assured, and determined. Where once we'd call a woman arrogant, what we see instead is assertiveness.

Now let me be clear: Betsy was by no means villainous. She was strong, assured, and determined; she was resilient and resourceful. But she was also, to me, a reminder about how we often view "negative" traits in a woman—and then dismiss any woman with these traits. Like I'd already noticed, Betsy brooked no fools; she had little patience for people who abused and abandoned animals, and her words could be vitriolic. They were not for polite company.

But they also served their purpose. Betsy was a refreshing reminder that genteel decorum wasn't always the right path when trying to give voice to the voiceless.

Bold-spokenness has its rightful place. Because what better way to judge our own humanity and heart than by the way we treat those who most need our help?

Ginger Cat

There's a dark Dickensian twist of fate suffered by untold legions of furry David Copperfields, little kittens born to the streets who live a cruel life. They're in for a post-Mama marathon of paw-to-mouth misery, which is pretty much cat hell on earth, but at least it's the cat hell they know and no other. On the contrary, those who are rescued (experiencing a tapas-sized taste of heavenly fat-cat happiness) and then cast back down into the forgotten-furball abyss once again are the truly tragic.

What *does* go through the minds of those two-minute Mother Teresas? How could they frivolously feed then forget

Fido or Fluffy with nary a blip on their radar? A fickle food bowl takes a terrible toll on the once-loved pets, as they strive to survive their roller-coaster plight of part-time/one-time pet turned family castoff. To experience even one mouth-watering morsel of food and love, then to be banished, alone, forgotten and desperate, is a crime not just against the animals themselves but against our very humanity.

Therefore, in the interest of nonviolent self-preservation, I've become very adept at sniffing out—and silencing—every imaginable kind of harebrained-heroism story that some do-gooder expects to unload on me. They often recount, with a lame flick of the wrist, their own monumental generosity. A half-eaten hotdog tossed to a little mama mutt with hungry pups in tow; plein air table scraps to a skin-and-bones tom. They are but Band-Aids on a broken life. What are these people thinking by planting such gut-wrenching images into my sad-critter-overloaded brain? That they will kneel while I knight them for their one-minute meddling? And yet, these stupid Samaritans are often clearly befuddled—and yes, bent out of shape—by my thinly veiled contempt for such shortsighted pseudo-benevolence.

No! They should be doing the right thing! Give Little Alley-Orphan Annie a lift to the local no-kill shelter, with a Benjamin or two to cover her room and board, or, better yet, take her home with you. What a nice souvenir for your badge of honor! A real-life, living, breathing kitty! Now *that's* something to brag about.

Chips guesses there is a law of conservation of stray-ache suffering. For all the flunkies who offload it with the distasteful deposit of a cat or dog on the side of the highway, there are people like me who absorb it. And, truth be told, I seem to have ever-growing gigabytes of gruesome bait-and-switch animal attachments, as my strays come and go. No matter the feel-good family unions I match up for my rescues, I still suffer from the here-today-gone-tomorrow tearjerker.

But once in a great while, I find myself with a different finale, a here-to-stay-happily-ever-after.

One north-of-ninety Mayberrian—a screw-all-the-birthdays Betty White acolyte—capitulated to her daughter's assumption she would be, soon enough, gray-to-gone and was thus whisked away from her world into her daughter's care. The graceful lady's alley cat friend had no such luck. Though the old lady had faithfully refilled her backyard buddy's bowl full of Friskies love, her family had (for some really wicked *un*reason) not planned for her ginger-colored cat. So when the kitty's white-haired heroine was put out to pasture, the alley cat was cut off cold turkey (or, well, *no* turkey). I got word of the *cat*astrophe from a tender heart who witnessed the tabby travesty (but was in no position to step up), so I packed up the little kitty, still prowling the vacated grounds in search of her vanished Lunch Lady.

Huddled in a dark corner of the cage, with as much no-cat's land between us as her new square footage allowed, she looked miserable. Every inch of her down-on-her-luck looks bespoke of a hard-knocks, hard-as-rocks life. Her ears were mincemeat, testament to a lurid list of alley altercations and Jack Frost's ghastly wintertime tattoos, and she was saturated in layers of grunge, a hopeless has-been hanging onto her memories of her cat-chow past. Despondent and despairing, she was in no mood for my usual BFF olive branch.

Instead, my overtures were met with a bloodcurdling *Back off, Blondie!* And accompanied by hair-raising hisses, spits, and a one-false-move-and-I'm-shredded-wheat left hook. With no hint of a bluff, by the way. I had on my hands one seriously suspicious little worrywart.

I could do this. I'd tamed dozens of kitties. I had my strategies. I knew my techniques. Yet, weeks later, after I'd bumbled through my whole bag of cat-charming tricks, we still weren't even close to polite speaking terms. She remained my terrified little terrorist, and only then did I begin to grasp the scope of work it would take to overhaul the fear in my supremely skeptical scaredy-cat.

I turned to my spare-pet reservist. Yes, Chips was perpetually overbooked, given his lawyer work with humans, but still I pleaded my case for his intervention. I was pinning my hopes on him discovering some secret entryway into that desperately frightened soul.

And so it was meant to be.

Ginger Cat and Chips started out as casual acquaintances, as I had once tried to be, but Chips had the patience of a saint. He would idle away countless hours parked on the floor of the bedroom, just hanging out, holding up the walls. Whatever book he brought, he'd read aloud, to get her used to his voice. After a month or so, he escalated his efforts. He brought in a cat toy, an extended pole with a feather on the end, that proved to be the perfect icebreaker. Still, he dared not touch her; there would be no petting this psycho-puss. Until suddenly she plopped, nonchalantly, into Chips's lap like the most routine lovey-dovey cuddles. Shocked, Chips wouldn't move, not daring to disrupt this major philosophical breakthrough with even the most unmenacing of twitches. There he remained, session after session, with a ferocious cat on his lap, kneading (and badly scratching up) Chips's legs. With his one pair of pants shredded that first surprise time, he would always return wearing at least three layers between her claws and his thighs.

All the while Ginger was plumping up. She was getting used to the good life, bellying up to the Blue Buffalo bar, and soon we discovered a downside to our little lazybones's backside. Since she would now allow Chips, her only friend, to run his fingers through her fur, he came across a big, knotted mass of hair on her butt, the result, we presumed, of a now-fat-cat issue with grooming. The heinie-strangling hair weave had to go. But how, if we wanted to keep all our fingers and toes? Even Chips, to whom she would deign a touch, could never have snipped off the offending fur without shedding his own blood.

Heavy sedation was our only hope. Since snare nets and tranquilizing darts seemed imprudent for us amateurs, we went with dispensing the dope into her dinner. Yet Ginger, we discovered to our dismay, could and would ignore any slightly piquant psychotropic seasoning in her canned cuisine. Day one of our daring DIY project produced zero interest in her newly flavored meal. Ditto for day two. We would have to ditch our efforts to untangle her unhealthy fur; we couldn't let her starve. Yet on day three, Ginger chose to nibble the sleepyhead stew. A fog slowly crept over her, and Chips prepped for the procedure. Bravely he commenced the snarl surgery, anticipating nine rounds of mayhem, even with the sedative. Yet Ginger remained docile and pliant as Chips snipped away. Mission Knot-Impossible accomplished.

Relieved, I tiptoed in to see them, and, to my great surprise, my once-growling gremlin had miraculously transformed into a warm-and-fuzzy purring pet—even long after the sedation had worn off! Ginger was ready for cat company. She'd mellowed, for sure, though any unpredictable human endeavor still wrought inconsolable pussycat Armageddon panic.

No finding a new forever home for her, then. Given all the people pleasers overflowing in every shelter, Ginger's stick-in-the-mud personality would go over like a lead balloon. Our matchmaking odds for her were beyond bleak, so we soon came to accept that only a *way* laid-back life in the Pauly commune would keep our shy girl's fear at bay.

Could a four-pawed friend be found among our own critters instead? Would Mrs. Chippy or Tiger Lily, fellow alley-cat expats, step in with some welcome-wagon hospitality?

First, we had to get her from the second-floor bedroom up to the third-floor attic. We closed up all the rooms on the second floor. Chips put up a barrier to the staircase from the first floor, and then we opened the door to the third floor. Finally, we opened the door to Ginger's bedroom and moved out of the way. Well, curiosity didn't kill the cat, but it did get her out of the room and onto the stairs heading up to the third floor. With that, Chips slammed the door shut. Ginger was now in Cat Land.

I fretted. How well would this truly work? In hindsight, we had no reason to anticipate any bold alliance building. Luring Ginger from her tidy little fiefdom into a giant maze of a space with foreign kitties prowling around was a complete roll of the dice. Chips had encouraged plan B pragmatism, given that I've been known to veer off into daydream-believer delusional territory, but still, I clung to my great expectations that Ginger would bond with . . . somebody.

And would you believe it? Inexplicable cosmic forces propelled my onetime terrorist onward and upward and into the welcoming paws of my other humble homesteaders. Over the cat-clogged years of presiding over my whiskery psych ward of maladjusted misfits, I'd *never* seen such instantaneous all-for-one-and-one-for-all formation of feline friendship. Without a blink, the other cats welcomed Ginger into their tightly knit tribe. Ginger reciprocated, exposing an ardent adoration for Tiger Lily, the baby of the bunch. From that magic moment, Chips relinquished his only-friend status in favor of Ginger's new kitty crush. Now we would see a blissful curl of orange and white around Tiger Lily, a fluffball of furry love.

Any good writer understands the importance of evolution in a scene. If there is stagnation in a chapter, we risk losing the reader. If the events are important enough to record, they must have a purpose. How will the action—and its emotional impact—alter the story going forward? So we look at the beginning, then we look at the end; how has our protagonist changed?

Betsy was drafting her stories when they came to me, but however rough some of her scenes might have been, I love "Ginger Cat" for the clear-eyed evolution we see. In the beginning, Betsy is steaming mad, anger and frustration dripping from every word at the carelessness and heartlessness of humans who can toss away, ignore, abandon, or neglect the pets that were either once in their care or should have been. She is righteous and indignant and justifiably so. Our less-than-tactful heroine spits fire at the injustices of animal welfare, a woman on a tirade, a woman on a mission. She offers a critique, generalized as it is, but then we see her change, evolve. No, she does not temper her anger at the irresponsible humans, but she does one better. With the softening of her tone, she turns us, the reader, inward. ***Here, let me show you just how rewarding cat rescue can be.*** She takes us from a place of vitriol to an experience of devotion and love. Yes, she tells us, it's not easy, but these little creatures, whose hearts melt our own, deserve all the love and care we can provide.

And ***that*** is how we see a righteous fury, often mislabeled as signs of a troublemaker, stripped away to reveal a person's soft, warm center.

Betsy was no villain; Betsy, she would herself argue, was no hero. But villain or hero or anything in between, Betsy was all heart.

A defining characteristic in a friend, wouldn't you say?

Chapter 10

In my writing classes, I preached what I did not practice. ***Observation***, I would impart, ***is essential. Look around,*** smell ***around. Keep your eyes and ears and nose and fingers and toes and every other sense and organ open to what's around you.***

Sounds good, right? I believe it, I do. I wholeheartedly agreed with my own wisdom, yet I, myself, was neglectful. If I encouraged my students to carry around a tiny notebook in which to record their observations, my own pockets were empty. Though every writer has their own process, and there's no right or wrong way to write, still, I recognized the value of my advice for my own writing, so my lack of observational skills was a failing I was determined to rectify. (Not to mention my students were—rightfully—calling me on my own hypocrisy!)

It wasn't an animal, like for Betsy, that drew my attention when I finally started ***paying*** attention. It was a man. Old, likely into his seventies (though "old" is relative, yes? If one is ninety, then seventy is young, another observational assumption about which I should be wary). Nevertheless, the man, with sparse white hair, and a face full of wrinkles, a man who upon first glance seemed frail because he held onto the bars of the shopping cart in the parking lot with white-knuckled ferocity, suddenly skipped a few steps, picked up speed, and jumped on the bottom of the cart with the abandoned glee of a child. With the momentum of his downward trajectory, the man rode the cart all the way to his car. He then gingerly stepped off, loaded his groceries into his trunk, and returned the cart like any other responsible adult. If he was aware of any additional attention—like from me or other bystanders—I have no idea. He himself seemed unobservant, a man in his own cheerful world, as he whistled his way back to his car.

I stared, long after the man had driven away. The cart ride had lasted only a few seconds; had I been loading my own groceries, perhaps I would have missed it. But then, I corrected my own faulty thinking. Before my observation lesson, loading groceries or not, I'm pretty sure I would have missed it. I would have, as usual, been in my own head (though not quite so cheery a place as the old man's inner world seemed to be). I might have caught the cart's movement out of the corner of my eye, but would I have *noticed*? I suspect not.

I dutifully reported, with awe and wonder, back to my class the next day.

This is what you see when you truly look, I proclaimed.

It was a lesson Betsy herself had long ago learned—if she had had to learn it at all. Because according to Chips's description of Betsy's "straydar," she had an innate ability to see what most of us could not. If I had to work at my observational skills—and we're talking me learning to notice the obvious movement of a full-sized man riding a grocery cart—Betsy just had them.

Despite the challenges Betsy's strays would sometimes bring her, those observational skills were nonetheless a gift.

Rounding Up Rovers

Rounding up roadside Rovers isn't exactly a walk in the doggy park. One must dodge distracted speed-demon drivers, and one must stalk disoriented dogs darting into the street who—can you believe it?—do not look both ways before crossing. And, with no room for error—no bumper-free buffer zone in case of any false move—one must tiptoe around freaked-out, famished Fido to tempt him off the blacktop with any bait at hand.

One such pup started as a fuzzy black spot at the edge of my vision, my usual blur given I'm always running late. I had to stop, lured by the mutt onto an old patch of pavement passing as a parking lot for a nearby diner, a mom-and-pop shop catering to the steady stream of 18-wheelers. A few has-been houses surrounded it, dwarfed by the endless foothills long past their mining glory days. All in all, it was a categorically un-Fido-friendly moonscape. And there, stretched alongside the highway, like he was sunning poolside, was a lap-sized dog. He was all alone, yet he seemed immune to both my twenty-question monologue and my manner of sugary small talk. He did have a lustrous coat and a plump privileged-pooch physique, so the band around my heart loosened, but still I was worried. His deaf indifference and less-than-ideal lounging location spurred me toward the mini-mart next door. I was not hopeful of any fruitful findings, armored as I was in well-seasoned skepticism. Not to mention my own appearance, my lady-about-to-lunch look, stuck out like a sore thumb among the caffeine-by-the-bucket customers. Nonetheless, I persevered, and over the chattering checkout din, I shouted my plea for any leads about the pup. Silence fell over the tattoo-and-testosterone-heavy crowd as dozens of steely eyes turned my way. Who *was* this strange, strappy-sandaled city slicker hollering at the top of her lungs?

And then, *thank you, Lord!* A gospel choir of true believers raised the roof with a mountain of testimonials singing the praises of that mongrel dog. I was able to piece together an endearing Cinder-fella scenario. The mysterious loiterer, it turned out, was a loyal lawn ornament and lunch-line mascot. Since his silent street-side debut, he'd graciously accepted all gestures of goodwill—especially of the gastronomic kind. He did shy away from petting of any kind, since no one among the band of brusque-talking 10-4 good buddies had yet laid a loving hand on him, but he was theirs nonetheless. He would indulge in a sunup-to-sundown sit-in each and every day, then would disappear into the night.

I thanked them all, accepting their knuckle-numbing handshakes; then I congratulated the furry fan-favorite on his doting human entourage and bid him adieu.

This small-time pit stop, hardly a pinprick on any map, had proven to be a mecca of humanitarianism. Here were a group of regular people taking in that small life under their many wings.

I must admit I cried as I pulled out of that parking lot, rejoicing for once, at the rare bit of goodness in my rearview mirror.

The incident got me thinking about dogs. They truly do wear the worst poker faces, don't they? They spell out their emotional moods like neon signs, complete with panting pantomimes. *Did someone say* treats? *Walk, walk,* walk? *Let's go, let's go,* let's go! *Oooh, YESsssss! Scratch riiiiight* there! They show us goo-goo-eyed gazes of undying love and despondent goodbye-till-five puppy eyes of despair. They are barking billboards who let it all hang out. So when I come across poor, lost hounds, their misery is abundantly evident. *Where the* heck *is my human? Please, please,* please *let me into your pack! Are* you *Alpha? I'm* starved, *what's for dinner?*

I wonder how it is that we're allowed crystal clear access to those K9 souls while our cats meter out their bank-vaulted POV in miserly dribs and drabs. Without favoring felines any less, I find a person's friendliest Best Friend all the more endearing for his cerebral Saran-Wrap. (And if my sneaking suspicions about reincarnation hold a drop of holy water, Chips was surely never a dog in any former flesh-and-blood format. In spite of a strong pack-man sense of lupine law and order, and a constant craving for the comforts of his own den, Chips just doesn't jive with the high fives and willy-nilly silly of a dog. Instead, he exudes the dignified King-of-our-Jungle reserve.)

But I adore the jubilance and canoodling of those superglued sidekicks. Yes, they demand incessant cradle-to-grave needs. Sure, dogs dig big black holes halfway to hell, slobber, stink and tinkle like barking babies, scratch and sniff and poop in all the wrong places, gulp down anything and everything remotely edible (and horrifyingly inedible), and work themselves into a lather over doorbells and deliverymen, but they have so doggone much fun while they're at it!

It's a lesson for all of us—how to soak up the joy of the smaller moments. Or, like two of our rescues showed us, how to soak up the uproariously, side-splitting good humor of the everyday.

The dogs had been sitting on the side of the road like a couple of sad tossed-out toys when I found them. They were wearily waiting for their dog-dumping daddy. No surprise, my door-to-door routine turned up nada. So, as usual, they came home with me. My offer was rewarded with a facial of salivary gratitude as I juggled that riot of blond fur and bicycling feet into the passenger's seat. Of course, they desperately tried to join me behind the wheel to pilot our ride home. Energetic doesn't even begin to describe the triple-A Energizer bunnies. The two were clearly birthday buddies, though of disparate paternity. (Mama got around, it seemed.) They were both Chihuahua-seasoned, where the brother, Peter, wore a Brillo-pad buzz cut while his sister, Hannah, was Goldilocks-glam.

When I got home, the two of them, in cahoots, exploded into a tornado of canine chaos. Yet again, I worried about spousal apoplexy, fearing that Chips would get angry over yet another mob of squatters encamped in his happy home. But yet again, my concerns evaporated when Chips walked in. He was immediately swarmed by a pair of pups dancing a frantic high-ten cha-cha looking for this latest human's bark of approval.

Chips just laughed. Amused, he scooped up a wiggle worm under each arm and even turned the other cheek for a two-tongued beard bath. Chips set them down, where, firing on all cylinders, the dogs were revved up and ready to go. They hit the ground at full gallop, two streaks stampeding in a ricocheting riot of yip and zip. The explosive invasion even sidelined our own flabbergasted furballs. Daisy Mae, queen of hair-raising, high-decibel barking, was actually left *arf*-less by those supersonic pip-squeaks.

If laughter was the best medicine, then we were getting full double doses.

Triple doses, actually, because we welcomed one more highly contagious smile-maker who was as light at heart as the rioting half-twins already bouncing off the Pauly Pound walls.

Only, he was much, much bigger.

And human.

Big Phil, aptly named, was a man full of humor, without the tiniest trace of mean. His infamous (and oft-quoted) Phil-isms, a droll playbook of life-is-good ground rules, sum up that great man's simple game plan:

- Spills are inevitable (mop it up and move on).
- The louder the music, the better the party (live out loud).
- One rule of carpet laying (and life): fuzzy side up.

Phil and the tiny tornados were matches made in humor heaven. Our don't-worry-be-happy human would definitely meet his match in those fun-for-all-and-all-for-fun canines. That was why Chips ensured Phil was at ground level (the easier for a tongue-bath facial, of course) while I retrieved the maniacs who had been recharging their doggy-Duracells in the laundry room. The two wind-up toys sprang to life.

They busted loose from my grip and pounced on our mountainous friend like he was a rodeo ride. The party pups, in a frantic, joyous frenzy, covered every last inch of Phil's irresistible immensity with whiskery kisses. Ringside, Chips and I howled through hysterical tears as the two mutts raged on.

It was one of those rare little iridescent moments, a taste of perfect joy.

Both Peter the Bold and Little-Miss-Goody-Two-(+Two)-Shoes Hannah had happy endings. Peter marched into a mutt-happy clan crowded with equally energetic kids, while Hannah filled four empty arms from a couple desperate to fill their waning dog days. They had lost their old doggy BFF ("the finest friend to ever walk this earth," they explained, choking up) and were looking for a new Queen of the Family Room. They were ready for the fireball that was Hannah, and I never counted a single can't-sleep sheep second-guessing that trio. Later, I was lucky enough to get pictures. Hannah, their lucky little couch-potato princess, was serenely perched between her smitten humans, all three of them aglow in adoration.

Years after my man-riding-a-grocery-cart moment, I still remember the bubble of joy I felt at seeing the old man. I remember I smiled, and I laughed. I remember I stopped. I took a moment, watching him play. We don't often do that—play, or stop to watch others play. Nor do we often stop to remember those moments after they've passed. But Betsy did. She observed and recorded what was most important to her. Phil and the dogs playing together were etched in her memory, a forever moment she wouldn't forget.

Observational skills, I began to understand, weren't necessarily about seeing things we hadn't seen before, nor were they just about becoming more aware of our environment. They were about tuning into the emotions of the moment. They were about seeking out one of those rare little iridescent moments. They were about savoring a taste of perfect joy.

Chapter 11

I am a cynic, the pessimist in my household and the harbinger of doom. If there is a rainbow, it's because the streets are impassibly flooded with rain. If there is sunshine, it is the kind that burns. If there are roses, they will be wilting; lollipops too sour. If there is a silver lining, it is because of a dark cloud.

And then I read "Oliver's Tale."

It seems that optimism originates from rainbows and roses, sunshine and lollipops.

And break-your-heart stories with effervescent endings.

Oliver's Tale

Oliver's tale is my own winsome canine counterpart to Mr. Dickens's dewy-eyed boy. It recalls the melancholy meanderings of a most unfortunate youth. It is a tale filled with roughshod characters and dastardly misdoings, yet redeemed by a majestic finish for our gentle hero as he finally finds his house of wall-to-wall puppy love.

One time on our way back to Mayberry after a dose of big-city Dallas fun, I spotted a black mound on the side of the road. Reflexive dread reared its ugly head; I was terrified it was a flattened Fido. But then I broke into a wide, sunny grin at the sight of the upright animal. He was a mysteriously diluted black Lab, stoically awaiting the return of his (expletives-deleted) dumper. He was a lost little lamb, the poor bedraggled boy, so he meekly allowed me to nudge him into the car. Instantly, he fell into a sleep that neither bumps nor horns could disturb. That ninety-mile nap and a fistful of Cheetos refueled my new orphan, waking up his charisma.

As always, I went over my new find, now named Oliver, with a fine-tooth flea comb and got him ready for his forever family. My matchmaking turned up a taker, a repeat customer, in fact. They had already adopted one of my alley-cat aristocracy and were now looking to add a dog to their playlist. Since Fluffy fit so well, I assumed an equally airtight forever for Oliver.

Alas, that record-setting sendoff proved to be among my all-time worst. Oliver was quickly reported MIA, having wandered away through the very-much-non-Snoopy-proof fencing. The reaction of his eight-day-old family? *Oh well, better luck next time*. That disposable dog dedication dispelled any hopes of family ties strong enough to stir up even the most lazy-boned search and rescue. And *my* search-and-rescue plans—more like a five-alarm fire! A blitzkrieg and a door-to-door doggy dragnet (of course!) were dissed by a shoulder-shrugging dog-mom. Nor would they make any plans to upgrade their fencing. And so, unbeknownst to those pretend pup parents, I put out my own APB.

And got an immediate hit. It turned out that one magic word—*reward*—grabbed the paper-reading public by their wallets. I trotted over to my runaway and met Oliver's accidental benefactor, who loved the idea of keeping him. After a few vague minutes of talking with him, and irrationally taken in by his craving for canine companionship, I agreed. I was certain that this warm-and-fuzzy welcome for my clueless tramp would guarantee a solid, amiable friendship, so I left my footloose protagonist at Door #2.

That was twice now I'd forgone my usual adoption scrutiny, so in headshaking hindsight, it was no wonder the whole disaster spiraled down into deeper doggy doo-doo. Though in my crystal ball–less defense, only a fortune teller could have foreseen the terrible transformation wrought upon that once-lucid man by meth madness.

My "trouble" antennae went on Code (seeing) Red after I called Oliver's latest landlord for a follow-up and had to suffer through an indecipherable exchange. A not-so-friendly kennel call confirmed the horrific needle-powered nosedive of Oliver's human and its heartbreaking K9 fallout. My former puppy-chow poster boy now cowered in the corner of a ramshackle pen, avoiding eye contact with his menacing pit bull–plus playmate (or not?). The two had only a single shelter, a small crawlspace under the house of many horrors—and you can guess who got first dibs. Every last blade of green in Oliver's prison yard had given up the ghost, trampled by caged-beast pacing and uncollected poop. There was hardly a slurp of swampy water in the lone bowl.

Oliver's dog daddy, once dapper and firing on all cerebral cylinders, was altered beyond recognition. He was now a bleary, barely-there zombie, only slightly sobered by mad-as-hell me. With a faint glimmer of guilt, he wisely forfeited Oliver back to the land of the living. His newer object of neglect, the second dog, had fared a fraction better, no doubt beating out my lovebug for the occasional bag of food with one make-my-day snarl.

I confiscated the most damning dog-wrecker evidence I could, praying for some slim hope of dead-head redemption. I took a deep breath and read Dopey the riot act, twice. Hazily he ingested my Good-K9-Housekeeping checklist, and then he mumbled a tepid assenting grunt to get his remaining dog act together. Sadly, despite plenty of prods on my part to kennel "cops," the man was getting no comeuppance. Their drive-by spy denied seeing any alleged dog dungeon, so I turned the numbskull—and his train wreck of a life—over to the real pet police. When I drove away, I was relieved beyond measure at Oliver's second salvation. Still, I vowed full-on, proper, paranoid, uber-prudence next time, to prevent any more screwups in finding Oliver a home.

My underfed underdog still had managed to sprout into his oversized appendages during his Nightmare-on-Stoner-Street incarceration. Thankfully, there were happier times ahead. Ever milquetoast-timid tempered, Oliver was nonetheless socially stunted after his purgatory. He was a roly-poly mischief maker with enough girth to bring down the unsuspecting human in a body-slam greeting. Not to mention he needed a lengthy refresher course in proper gentlemanly grass-going. Training was, therefore, *re*training, which, yes, tried me, the trainer, terribly, but the dear boy's earnest efforts and genuine tail-between-the-legs remorse acquitted all carpet indiscretions.

Finally, Oliver passed his final *pet*iquette PhD(og) exams with distinction. We were up for round three.

Would it be the long-awaited charm?

The head of an area nursing home had responded to my glowing Wonder-Dog-Seeks-Super-Hero-Humans want ad. She had already welcomed feathered friends into the nursing home for the residents, and finned friends, too. She was ready to take on a dog.

Oliver was the leading candidate. I'm sure it was his superlative barking-ambassador credentials (or maybe my unconditional doggy-back guarantee) that ticked all the boxes on her coworkers' wish list: a junior social director with proven mix-and-mingle skills, some polished dance moves, and natural comedic timing. But given the white-glove caliber of this job prospect, I wanted to ensure I drilled Oliver in preparation for his face-to-(furry)-face interview. I worked to erase any last hint of deal-breaker wrestling holds and call-of-the-wild bolts. Still, I was nervous as I drove him to his audition. His sordid hardships weighed heavily on my heart; I so wanted to make it right this time.

Oliver received a hero's welcome, to my relief. The residents clambered to lay hands on my life-of-the-party pal. Mr. Extrovert himself immediately basked in that onslaught of 360-degree smothering, angelically posing for endless pats and praise. Instantly, he won over the nurses with his tantalizing (albeit wildly indiscriminate) I-love-*you*-best kisses and nuzzles. My canine Casanova and all his baby-lamb canoodling was a hit.

The Boss Lady was awed by Oliver's top-dog command performance. She signed him on for full-time wags. It was a rare jewel box home of nonstop puppy love, perfect for Oliver, but still, passing his leash struck me with a rush of tears. I was sure he was finally in good hands, but still, "goodbye" stuck in my throat as I gave the lucky guy one last hug.

Soon I would learn I had nothing to fear.

Our displaced, misplaced, and monstrously mismanaged boy had finally found his forever home, and his happy ending only got happier as he quickly got the hang of his great big new gig. Oliver had been hired for a nine-to-five workday, spending his Milk-Bone breaks under the nurses' desks (you sly dog, you) and lounging off-duty in a deluxe outdoor den. Yet within a week, the celebrity apprentice had so endeared himself with his charm and impeccable decorum that he was given round-the-clock carte blanche to roam freely among his devoted fan club. His brand-new backyard bachelor pad was quickly abandoned as the resident rock star now slept with vying groupies elatedly making mattress room for those sprawling sixty pounds. His human coworkers were equally lovestruck, and the only problem seemed to be not enough of Oliver to go around.

On a veterinary visit some months later, I bumped into the irrepressibly happy Oliver. He was with another impish pup, the second canine counselor-at-large "hired" by the nursing home. I had to smile; it had been *my* big buddy's popularity that paved the way for this new dog, and I was so proud. Given the tumult that Oliver had experienced, and knowing he still had a heart untarnished by miseries, my faith was restored. Where my expectations of the world had faded, Oliver's exuberance was an instant tonic to brighten my days.

Friends, we often assume, share common interests. Personality traits, too. One recognizes a kindred spirit if one spots a similar quirk among one's friends. Commonalities mean connection. Yet this story proved the complete opposite. It is difficult for me to share Betsy's enthusiasm, optimism, and positivity—despite her choice words to the meth man—but through Oliver's tale, I could live it. I could feel her anger at Oliver's mistreatment, the bubbling pain of injustice, and I could feel Betsy's choking sadness at her tearful goodbye, but I could also feel not just her joy but her renewed hope. If Oliver's ending was a tonic to brighten Betsy's world, Betsy offered me the same.

And when one often lives behind clouds of gray, one can more readily welcome rays of yellow sunshine.

Chapter 12

I almost stopped reading when I came to Betsy's chapter she called "The Calculus of Cat Catching." The alliteration was amazing. The title was titillating. It promised good-hearted humor and hijinks. Given Betsy's warm, self-depreciating tone throughout her manuscript so far (albeit alleviated with sharp barbs at those who deserved them), I should have had no reason to pause.

Yet there was that word. *Calculus*.

I shivered.

You know how you're not supposed to diss math so the young people in your life, especially girls, don't get turned off the subject?

Yeah . . . no.

Math and I don't get along. *Calculus* was my enemy number one. I feared it with all my heart, soul, mind, and body. Literally, I would shake walking into calculus class in high school. But there I was, forced to face my foe. I didn't want to; I had dreams of a lustrous, luminous literary career; why would one want to waste one's time on frivolous subjects such as calculus?

"To keep your all your doors open, Jennifer," my engineering-professor father lectured.

"But when do I get to *close* the damn doors?" I countered. I really never wanted to walk through them—either physically through the classroom door at school or practically by dealing with anything math-related in the big, wide real world.

Yet still a minor, I had no choice. There were the Ontario curriculum requirements to graduate from high school, and then there were the Braaksma requirements. I was to complete a senior science and a senior math course. End of story. My poor engineering-professor father had to concede defeat on my aptitude in science. When my grade 11 chemistry teacher asked if I was taking the senior course and I said no, he said, "Good." When I got 8 percent on my first grade 12 physics test (yes,8, as in a single-digit score), my poor teacher despaired. I'm positive he passed me in the course with a 50 percent just because he was the nicest man on the planet (and didn't want to have me in his class again). So, no, science and I were not a match. My well-meaning (yet misguided) father held out hope for math.

To be fair, I'd actually done well up until grade 11. In fact, an alien had taken over my brain for my first two years of high school because I managed to complete the courses quickly and was ready for calculus by my junior year. Then my own brain came online, and, well, that was the end of that. I ***begged*** my dad to let me drop the course before I could fail it. I *did* have grades for university to consider. With a sigh (and with tittering laughter from my "I'm-staying-out-of-this" mother), he relented: "Only if you take it next year." Yes! Done! I had grand plans to weasel my way out of calculus before then. I had great faith in myself.

My father was a more formidable opponent than I had expected. He was immovable in my senior year. "You will take calculus. For your own good," he assured me. "I'm watching out for you," he placated. "I want you to have every opportunity," he enthused.

I. Did. Not. Want. Every. Opportunity.

But I was a dutiful daughter. I tried. I really did. A year older, a year wiser. Surely I could buckle down and learn this damn math. I mean, I had my own private tutor in my engineering-professor father.

By midterm, he gave up.

I really couldn't get it.

With the biggest sigh of relief heard around the world, I was finally allowed to drop it.

And you know what? I did okay without it. I had a high-average graduating high school, I was accepted into Canada's most prestigious journalism program, and I had earned a scholarship. Not bad for someone who couldn't figure out math or science.

So why, then, would I freeze up at Betsy's title, ***when she was talking about cats?*** I had no delusions. I knew the story wasn't about my dreaded nemesis, the math class that conquered me. Betsy was being cute, no doubt. A fun way to indicate she'd be talking cat-catching strategy.

But I stilled, because as much as Betsy's optimism was the prime opposite to my pessimism, I accepted that difference between us as a breath of fresh air. We may be nothing alike in that regard, but I could admire and appreciate her trait. I could see and appreciate the value of bighearted thinking.

But could I be friends with someone who so easily and ephemerally threw out the name of my worst enemy? I balked, not because the story was about math but because maybe, just maybe, Betsy was ***comfortable*** with math. It's a ridiculous notion to fear. No doubt she ***was***. She had a degree in business administration after all. She'd had a successful corporate career. She was able to successfully market her own art, an incredibly envious talent of most creatives I know.

But to me, one little word made me wonder if maybe we weren't alike after all. Maybe we would never have related to each other.

Maybe we would never have been friends.

It sounds crazy, I know. I once tried to explain to my kids how my thought process works. "I go deeper," I said.

"What does that mean?" my youngest asked.

"Okay, so you know how it snowed today? And Dad hasn't yet cleaned out the garage to park his car inside, so now his car on the driveway will be covered with snow and ice and freezing rain and he'll have to take a long time to scrape it off tomorrow?"

My girls nodded.

"Well, I notice the snow, and then I think about the consequences of the snow, and then I think about how Dad hasn't had time to clean out the garage because he's been so busy at work, and then I think that, well, I'm not ***quite*** so busy, so maybe *I* should have made time to clean out the garage to help him, and then I wondered if maybe I'm not doing enough to support him, and therefore maybe I'm not being a good wife."

My kids gawked at me. "You got 'you're not a good wife' because you noticed snow?"

I nodded, smiling. I wasn't truly worried about being a good wife (if he wanted to clean out his side of the damn garage before it snowed, then he should have made time!); it was just an example of how I can go deep.

Which is what I was doing with Betsy's one word. *Calculus*. Of course there was no rationale or logic to my thought process. I knew that. (I've lived with my brain for a long time; I'm aware of its quirks.) Still, I'm also aware of my own emotions. They were my own insecurities rearing their heads. It wasn't about calculus or math or even anything specific to Betsy's story. It was a deep, emotional fear that, like with calculus, maybe I wasn't good enough. Maybe Betsy would never have been my friend, had we met in earlier days.

So no matter how irrational or illogical, I went into this story with a bit of trepidation. I really, really wanted to keep relating to Betsy.

The Calculus of Cat Catching

Our salvaged cats are scrappy survivors. Only the toughest Tiny Toms and wiliest Miss Mittens graduate beyond Mama's tender care into the urban jungle of alleys and gutters. (Unclaimed country cousins have their own crosses to bear, scraping by on field mice and barnyard begging, but I'm an urban Ellie Mae.)

Just as other saintly mothers the world over, tabbies devote every waking hour to the betterment of their young, while footloose "fathers" (in the very vaguest biblical sense of the word—in matriarchal catdom, the menfolk are strictly sperm donors) live the stereotypical swinging single guy's life (albeit a woefully hardscrabble version). He grabs a quick bite wherever he can, engages in perpetual pissing contests and he-man headbutting with other over-hormoned Toms, Dicks, and Harrys, and spreads his glorious seed far and wide without a backward glance. Springtime revs up Mr. Macho's libido into overdrive, violently vying for every fertile Fluffy in his vicinity and then duking it out with that same oversexed fight club as he collects battle tattoos—interpretively etched ears and snouts among other bodily divots. (I'll never forget one broken-down old back-alley brawler, sprawled out roadside on a long-past New Year's Eve, finally throwing in the towel after his last wretched mile. Every inch of his barely-there being bore witness to a life sentence spent doing hard time. And a mega-tumor erased any last chance of a happy ending. He was put out of his misery, loved at least through those last hours, a painful reminder of all the other lost little ninth lives along the way.)

The setting sun brings out all my fellow night owls, as the undercover critters tiptoe from shrubs, sleeping Chevys, or, in the case of a Cain-and-Abel pair crossing my path one bitter cold evening, storm sewers. I'd just turned down a deserted side street in the shadow of our courthouse when the crunching of my tires on new-fallen snow alerted a wooly gray something or other. I saw its outline in the glare of my headlights. Coon-sized but cat shaped, he scurried back down to his basement apartment as I crept along. For an instant, two glowing orbs studied my slow-motion progress, and then, poof, he was gone into that secret subterranean world. With a sigh, and clinging to a forced philosophical inevitability, I dragged out my high-mileage Havahart cat cage once again.

The nocturnal solitude of our sleepy village, devoid of high-spirited nightlife, provided the perfect backdrop for collecting its most reclusive homeless inhabitants. My vintage pickup truck—with in-your-face spay/neuter propaganda shouting across its backside—was a notorious feline-fetching fixture around town, known to loiter on any street at any hour. Mayberry's see-all-tell-all transparency carries a corresponding benefit of tolerance. In exchange for presenting as public-gossip fodder, I earned a passport for any bizarre behavior.

During that evening's catch-a-cat vigil, I was a discreet distance away from the occupied gutter. The frigid weather eliminated any worries that an ill-timed inquiry ("Whatcha doin'?") would spook my persnickety prey. But it also meant I could not leave my little engine idling for warmth while I waited. The cat, expecting his terrain to be deserted, would surely flee. So there I sat, as my car descended into subzero icemaker mode. I was mummified in winter gear, but still, I had to fight the cold.

It was a long night. I hunkered down as I was in the driver's seat, filling my watch with midwinter whiskery daydreams. I had begun to wonder if all my solitary sit-ins would qualify as some sort of Chicken Soup for the Stray Lady Soul. Normally, my stakeouts aren't quite so CPA-symposium boring, but this bone-chilling hunt was major-league monotony. I'd set my trap, but as time slipped by (along with feeling in my fingers), I began to fret in earnest. The cat food in the cage would soon turn into a stinky Popsicle, thus rendering it useless. And still no sign of my tom. Arctic time dragged by, minute by (slow-as-molasses-in-Siberia) minute, lulling me into a semi-trance. It was only the sound of my teeth chattering that kept me awake.

Suddenly, I saw movement!

The still life at which I'd been staring turned into some furry action with the appearance of the cat. He crept around the cage, a veritable kitty candy store, determined to blend into his blurry shadowland. He remained wary about the wonderous goodies within reach, as though he would stop at window shopping only. It was obvious he was teetering between ravenous temptation and well-seasoned street smarts, but still he held back.

Then *bam!* Up out of the dark abyss sprang another cat. The first tom took off, clearly put out by the brazen insurgent. Brutus, Cat #2, wasted no time pussyfooting around the treats, and in no time, my trap was filled.

Which, of course, alerted Cat #1. He was onto me. But I wouldn't leave him. My nagging critter-littered conscience compelled a do-over, however frozen or fruitless it might prove.

If there's no mathematical law yet recognized that quantifies the maddening formula of waiting time multiplied by uncomfortable circumstances and exponentially increased by one's degree of anxious anticipation, I now formally dub it the Calculus of Cat Catching.

During my second go-round that evening, I experienced all three vexing variables. Thanks to my wizened returning customer who knew my tricks, I was faced with open-ended overtime. The mercury was plummeting. And my anticipation was sky-high. I'd had one triumphant rescue that night; I would be damned if I let this one go. Yes, I was skating perilously close to loose-ends-are-for-losers lunacy.

But I was determined. I wouldn't blink, afraid that I'd miss the pair of night-vision eyes pointed my way. There! A shadow! Somehow, it turned into a cat. He was back, still propelled by an empty stomach. He treaded carefully, checking out the food in my trap, and then—*yes!* He was mine!

I'd won!

But oh, how cocky I was in my double victory. It blinded me to the epic saga to come.

We separated the two cats back at home. The first cat found (and second retrieved) remained highly suspicious about this whole House Pet thing, entirely unswayed by his posh, new climate-controlled accommodations and supply of deluxe snacks, so we ensured a few days of domestic decompression. Slowly, he surmised that his prison guards, Chips and I, harbored no ill will. He seemed prepared to acquiesce, in time, to a passing acquaintance. All the while buried deep under the guest bed well out of my most unwelcome reach, of course.

At such time that I could *finally* lay hands on the cat, we paid a call to the v-e-t (not daring to speak aloud such an anathema among our edgy little friend) for The Works. Sadly, there was just no way to prepare an unsuspecting rookie for the horrors awaiting within. (Even his bossy sewer buddy sang a very different tune under the stethoscope.) When I left him, he offered me the most pitiful backward plea, elevating my status from barely tolerated Lunch Lady to his Only Hope.

It was the last I saw of my bedraggled brown cat.

I came to collect my unhappy camper the next day. Immediately I recognized our battered cat carrier—every tom and his twenty-seven brothers had been in that plastic case before—as the vet tech emerged from the backroom bedlam. I peeked in to console my little shell-shocked convalescent—only to find someone else's cat glaring back at me!

Inside was a strange arctic-fox-furred glamour-puss.

"This isn't my cat," I proclaimed, declaring a mismatch.

This, naturally, sent the whole staff into a tailspin of missing-critter chaos. Finally, the laundress was summoned, pulled away from a poodle in full suds, since she would have been the last stop on my alley-cat overhaul assembly line.

She laughed. "I swear," she said, raising her right hand, "this is your cat."

I peered closer; could it be true? Could Mr. Fancy Pants here be my very own back-alley rescue? Well, look at that. Yes, this whiskered work of art was indeed my dirt-coated hobo, bathed twice and now reappearing as a ten-pound, pink-nosed cotton ball. A detailed inspection confirmed the same jagged ears; this Clark Kent/Superman was mine to take home.

From pouty Pigpen to parading Powder Puff, the cat's overnight reinvention as a purring pretty boy spawned unexpected narcissism. Oh, he would strut his stuff on the catwalk, trolling to and fro just to mesmerize me. Like any breathtakingly beautiful being, smothered in automatic oohs and aahs, Snowman, the cat's new name (Chips's idea) couldn't help but go Hollywood. (Hmm . . . Charlton Hiss-ton, Paul New-cat, Robert White-furred . . .) He would puff up as he coyly pranced and preened before his audience of one. And if I was absent, if there was no fussing and fawning, then Snowman would seek out any mirror to shamelessly strike a pose. He was a feline Adonis, staring at his stunning reflection with frank admiration. And I get that many cat-haters would claim exaggeration, that no doubt the cat had a face only a crazy cat lady could love, but trust me, that Cat Fanicer centerfold not only *was* that gorgeous, he knew it, too. A few weeks out of the sewers and my once-bedraggled beast was now fully cognizant of his aesthetic superiority. He was absolutely an unapologetic *purr*ima donna, wholeheartedly annoyed by the household pets around him and their damn distracting demands upon my time. It had to be all about Snowman.

I admit I fell under his spell, but despite my flagrant infatuation, I did attempt to deliver Mr. Cat-Trophy himself into an appropriately awestruck home of worshippers-in-waiting. However, Snowman the Snobbish had zero interest in expanding his social circle among—I was assuming he figured—the various oafs I presumptuously paraded past his royal nose. He would reemerge after each failed introduction and pin me with a withering glare. Clearly, he had no intention of relinquishing his throne.

It didn't help that I was already a loyal fan-servant, and Chips had to reluctantly acknowledge that Snowman was here to stay. It was, Chips knew, a fait accompli. There would be yet another wife-robbing interloper in his life.

But it turned out Snowman wasn't just a pretty face. He was cute *and* clever, so he took it upon himself to patch things up with the household's other human. Inevitably, Chips, too, succumbed to Snowman's winsome ways—to the point where he was seen chasing a four-pawed cloud through our corridors. Not long after that, Chips gained a new white shadow.

And Snowman's gutter mate? The one who swooped in for rescue first on that frigid winter night? He, too, thrived. He was burly to Snowman's fine features, but Mr. Mittens VII also had pristine teeth and clean bloodwork, a remarkable accomplishment in the viral cesspool of urban alleys. Our vet determined the two toms were the same age, and given their shared rivalry, I gave in to my imagination that they were the closest of kin.

Oh, they were birds of a feather, all right, though they had two distinctly different styles of staying put at the Paulys'. While metrosexual Snowman tap-danced around any hint of tooth-and-nail trouble, the big, gray bruiser bulldozed his way through every guest-room encounter. Mighty Mitt would cut us off at the pass, radically rearrange hairdos, and snare socks, all as if to say he wouldn't do well anywhere else. Of course he won the day. Our newest poster boy for Naughty Pets moved into the recently vacated penthouse, which became his exclusive stomping grounds. It didn't take him long to beef up to his twenty-pound fighting weight, and with a cat's exponentially superior power-to-package ratio, our whiskery warrior was a force to be reckoned with. Playtime inevitably escalated into anything-but-playful battle, and despite all our attempts at glossing over our embarrassing defeat in talking down tomcat terrorists, Mr. Bring-It-*On* just couldn't get through his giant head the idea that such wallop-now, ask-questions-later savagery was way out of bounds on his civilized new playing field. He remained every bit the alley gladiator.

Weeks and months melted away as Chips and I turned tiger-tamers. They'd been sentenced to the top floor as maximum-security inmates; could we calm them enough to parole them to whole-house privileges? It was tough love—and tough on us—but from sharing (shredding) the morning newspapers to late-night laughs (leg locks) with Jay Leno, we finally finagled good behavior out of them. To be honest, it was as much a matter of practicality as true optimism about their potential to be team pussycat players. It was tiring training.

But our old guard ended up tolerating big-boy Mitt with trademark blasé, seemingly secure as they were in their hierarchy and home-court advantage. It gave us the first fragile hope for a halfway-happy ending. Adding homewrecker number thirteen (!) to the herd was not my husband's idea of a fairy-tale finish. But Mitt learned quick. He gravitated to our all-male squad of varsity mischief makers, then trailed every tail-twitching move. He even exposed his tremendous underbelly in a submissive vulnerability, like the outsider hoping the jocks would invite him to join in their cat-nap-break carousing. And so they did.

Their top choice of activity became Mixed *Meow*shal Arts matches, our little macho-men's interpretive contact sport of choice. They would take on Mitt, mindful of his wooly-mammoth tonnage, with their usual silent bear dances of half-baked swatting diluted with haggard hugs. Though often, like tired old TV wrestlers, my old guys were usurped by Mitt's gung-ho winner-takes-all Mike Tyson moves.

Even with some fuzzy kind of fraternity in mind (maybe, maybe not), Mr. Mitt just didn't have the wherewithal (or wish) to dilute those testosterone-soaked Tough Guy tournaments down to sissy-cat skits. We grossly underestimated the need for a speedier reaction time as referees; our senior-citizen snail's pace was not exactly cutting it. We would hear a *what-the-heck* howl, or pass a vanquished, fleeing cat only to find Mitt standing center ring, waiting for another foolish partner to step forward. The nervous B-team benchwarmers wisely gave a wide berth around Mitt, the chokehold champ, but they also didn't noticeably shun him. In the end, it all seemed to be just ground-floor gang fun gone sideways.

Our female cats paid no heed to all that headbutting. Just like their supersized wild cousin-lionesses, they could civilly commingle among their sorority (with only petty squabbles over confiscated lounges, ear-licking inequalities, and jockeying for post position at the happy *pop* of the Purina can). Our toms were theoretically celibate, but the backstreet boys' libidos couldn't be entirely extinguished by the vet's knife. Still, they showed all due deference to the ladies (especially Chippy—you can take the cat out of the alley, but you can't always take the alley out of the cat). They would invite the female kitties for a quick game of tag, or a cozy pileup, but rarely would they insult their grande dame status with disrespectful shenanigans. Our matriarch, Ms. Sunshine, would preside over the pride with the cheerful authority of a seasoned Cub Scout den mother. Imagine our red-hot horror, then, weeks into Mitt's trial run, to hear a bloodcurdling uproar. We found Sunny in full cower next to the fur-thirsty culprit (his mouth clogged with orange evidence). Our arrival thwarted any real Red Cross carnage, but the sickening sight of our proud little queen cringing in terror put us on high alert to big trouble.

We didn't have to wait long for it.

Our older cat, Jimmy Mittens Jr., had, we'd discovered, a burdensome chip on his shoulder. Coaches would call it a piss-poor attitude, but what it amounted to was that Jimmy would read antagonism into every little sniff or sneeze, imprudently biting the brave hands that fed him as well as any other living thing pausing in his path. Maturity, time's natural Xanax, hadn't much mollified his half-empty outlook on life. Only her Royal Hissing Highness, Lil' Abner—packaged with plenty of *how-dare-you!* Siamese spit and vinegar—held her own with the barroom brawler. She'd warmed to Jimmy Mittens Jr. when he'd arrived years earlier, much to our head-shaking amazement. (And a good lesson reminder: Never, ever bet against a cat.) But more fragile kitty egos, painfully learning about Jimmy's lack of small-group skills, kept their distance. Hence, he had no bad-urge surge protector. What he had instead was no hesitation to mix it up over any vague threat to his catly manhood. No, Iron-Man Mittens created an airtight vacuum around his personal *you-talkin'-to-me?* space, within which only the truly courageous or clueless dared trespass.

Of course our original bad boy, Jimmy, would mix it up with Mitt, the beefy upstart rabble-rouser. *Of course* we should have seen that coming, but alas, only looking back through life's rearview mirror of regrets could we see the obvious.

As any (alleged) head-of-household well knows, depositing a stranger into other cats' already-neurotic midst always muddies the waters. Even when everyone is settled, it's never Caribbean-clear sailing. Always there are ever-swirling undercurrents of *meow*lodrama, which leaves someone's snout out of joint. Yet despite Mitt's troublesome warm-up rounds, we were woefully unprepared for the inevitable slaughter to come.

For a while, Jimmy had been prudently pussyfooting around Mitt the interloper. I confess it imparted in us a false sense of security. We were relying on our so-far, so-good, dull-as-preschool-scissors sensibilities. No doubt, there were subtle symptoms of venomous angst mutely brewing beneath the cool-cat calm, lost to our distracted humanness.

Supersonic speed is a cat's most mesmerizing and lethal talent. It was for that reason that the brutal melee was history before we could track down those hair-raising howls. Mitt, indefensible defendant, had his jaws chock full of telltale black tufts. He was smart enough to register our volcanic fury and made a hasty retreat. Jimmy, the nonplussed plaintiff, stood frozen in shock, affording us miraculously bite-free forensics. Here and there, divots of Jimmy's topcoat were missing, but a gaping gash on his neck—Mitt had literally gone for the jugular—was well beyond our First Aid kit.

By the end of the day, our roughed-up little Rambo returned home in surly disgust. He was shaved in a most unbecoming punk style, with a drainage tube sticking out of his newest orifice and the dubious addition of an oversized Elizabethan collar (the latter prevented the plucking of the former) *as well as* ample dosage of equally unwelcome meds.

As for Mitt, we didn't wait for his third fur-flying strike before locking him up into his penthouse cell. He'd earned his stint in kitty solitary confinement. Still, Chips and I were wary over the whole fiasco. Keeping peace within the Pauly commune of malcontents was a relentless tactical tilt-a-whirl. It took intestinal fortitude to face the dreadful necessity to scold—or squirt—a doe-eyed little *what, me?* waif. (A little sprinkle of water and these cats practically melted as if they were the Wicked Witch of the West.) Pet parenting was tricky business, but we were dredging up every last ounce of gray matter and gumption to take on the dark, dangerous side of Mitt.

A major overhaul was required, but we were at a loss, particularly when that broken-down cat poured himself all over our laps with his love-motor running. I didn't have a clue about his prospects for rejoining the cat herd, but I also couldn't throw in the tabby-taming towel and sentence him to a solitary existence—or no existence at all. Now in uncharted Bad Cat waters, I reached deep into the dwindling reserves of cures. Drugs. I'd roll the dice on Mitt with a magic pet potion.

Our puzzled pharmacist diplomatically requested clarification of the patient's name. Yes, Mr. Mittens Pauly VII was correct. Hesitantly, he dispensed the top-dollar dose of attitude adjusters Mitt needed and wished "Mr. Pauly" good luck. I muffled a chuckle and took pity on the poor man's confusion.

"He's our cat," I explained.

Our pharmacist laughed with an amused shake of his head. I had to smile, imagining the many Mayberry dinner table conversations that evening about the deranged beast and his all-out, she'll-do-anything benefactress.

Be that as it may, that precious little bottle of hope brought us a major miracle. Our meowing Mack Truck destruction gave way to a baby-lamb cat. Granted, giving Mitt his happy-camper pills was no cakewalk. It's the rare—okay, frankly fictional—cat who willingly submits to having a foreign object crammed into its mouth full of sharp-toothed weapons. I had experience in this fight. My old friend Mildred's cat Bunny was a sweet sloth of a kitty until it came time for her penicillin. Then, oh god, she turned into a show-stopping Cirque Du Deranged Cat acrobat, twisting and screeching away as I tried to hand-feed her the kitty candy. Her tantrums were epic. Now I was up against the same challenge—but with a cat who *wasn't* already sweet-tempered? What *was* I thinking?

But I had to do what I had to do, and so I went in, dosing my natural-born killer with as much speed and stealth as my slow motor skills could muster. The inevitable bites were rarely intravenous and always reconciled by both wronged parties with a kitty kiss and ruffled-feathers rubdown. Whatever hurt I experienced faded the moment I saw my reward: my fire-breathing cat-dragon back on all fours.

Don't forget that we were also still caring for Mitt's victim, Jimmy. His recuperation was lengthy and unpleasant for all (when Motor-Mouth Jimmy Mittens ain't happy, ain't nobody happy). Oh joyous day, when those Frankenstein accessories were finally removed, daily amoxicillin-boarding completed, and both Chips and I could breathe a sigh of relief.

Fast-forward many scratch-free months with Mitt until I scrounged up enough nerve to usher two other major cat fixer-uppers into his lonely lockdown. Both new cats were settling in for a multicalendar stay with their own bountiful cornucopias of eccentricities. One was Atticus Finch, an irrepressible madcap prankster, and the other was Kewpie-doll-cute Gretel (imagine Gloria Steinem, Greta Garbo, and Marie Antoinette all rolled into one Little Miss Pouty Puss). They were introduced to the now-calm Mitt, with mixed reviews. Atticus and Mitt hit it off like frat cats, two wild and crazy guys flying after each other in some amalgamation of steeplechase, rugby scrum, and that all-time feline favorite I'm-The-Mountain-Lion-And-You're-The-Unsuspecting-Hiker-Passing-Beneath-My-Clifftop-Lair.

Suspicious Gretel monitored their antics from the sidelines, occasionally ensnared in the furry free-for-all but rarely with good humor. Unfortunately, her peace was also interrupted by Mitt's ardent amorous overtures. In spite of surgical negation, the big guy was intimately attracted to his frigid floor-mate. It took her hiding in narrow nooks and kitty crannies to get away from Mitt. That and me giving the rowdy tomcat a pinch more saltpeter for the tone-deaf-to-*no*-ladies to finally put an end to all those heavy-pawed passes.

Of course, I continued to make my life complicated. Chips, it turned out, had a serious allergic reaction to winter—or any latitude requiring more than gym shorts and flip-flops—so we started to retreat to Florida. It was the start of our residential merry-go-round, where we would, indeed, round up all of our flock, all thirteen cats, and make the trek south, then back again. It was as if we were scrambling addresses at whim to chase the alchemic mix of perfect month-to-month weather, fun, and Chips's lawyerly logistics.

At last, paradise was found and, barring the to-and-fro with thirteen angry anarchists in tow (the very definition of Crazy-Cat-Lady behavior), our balmy winter wonderland was met with universal approval. The cats loved lounging in the open air with plenty of warm rays for the consummate sun worshippers. Not to mention the endless parade of bite-sized lizards to drive our zealous hunters half mad with pleasure. Their unparalleled enjoyment in pursuit of their dull-witted prey was only slightly dampened by Chips's displeasure over such a cruel blood sport. It's a dichotomy of all cat lovers, to see those angelic furballs of love, the laziest of lap warmers, suddenly possessed with a demonic killing frenzy, and Chips was no exception. The daily captures, with wiggling green tails protruding from immensely proud mouths, elicited expletives from a man otherwise incapable of the slightest harsh word for his furry entourage.

Our new on-the-move lifestyle also meant we had to reckon with Mitt and his still-quarantined company, Atticus and Gretel. They'd had a season of good sportsmanship under their sidelined belts. We determined they, too, deserved a taste of salt air and sunshine. And so, we paroled the trio of misfits back into semicivilized society, though we did dog their every move for any hint of their abominable alter egos. I did wonder what the rest of the cats thought about the reformation of Mitt, their former tormentor, but, in catlike fashion, they all went about their business with supreme indifference. Mitt's only nerve-rattling misstep was a solo skirmish when he swan-dived off the edge of the pool into the drink. In one awesome split-second about-face, he propelled his fully-doused twenty pounds out of the deep end like a NASA launch, gave his soaked paws a lick, and strolled away without a backward glance.

Given that I'd witnessed Daisy Mae's distraught ineptitude whenever she waded into water beyond her depth, always flailing in dogpaddle panic, I was impressed with Mitt's self-assured recovery. I was reminded yet again to never bet against those nine-lives Olympians.

As the seasons turned, our whole thirteen-feline herd migrated north and south according to Chips's personal thermostat. All was peace, love, and understanding. The kitty-calmer pills had finally turned Mitt the Menacing Maniac into Mitt the Mild-Mannered.

Does peace ever last, though?

No. Life is chock-full of uncertainty, where tragedy is tucked among flashes of glory and heartbreak is hidden between the blessedly boring minutiae.

So it was that one night, as I took one last bedtime count of my brood, I was suddenly, blindly, shockingly hit from behind by a wild beast. He lunged, and bit, then lunged and bit again, hell-bent on bringing me down. As I turned to face the enemy, now crouched in full *kill* frenzy, my dear little Lazarus, once risen from the depths of his animalistic grave, had reverted into a monstrous Mr. Hyde. The throbbing pain of my bloodied legs had nothing on my breaking heart. It was the end of my hope and the end of the line for our deranged friend. As desperate as I was to trust again, Mitt was too unpredictable. Too dangerous. There was no way we could lock him up forever; cruelty in response to cruelty was inhumane, and so, through defeated tears, I had no choice but to say goodbye to our onetime-gentle soul. And only then were Mitt's demons finally gone.

Life is not a fairy tale, no matter how I'd love to believe otherwise, and especially not with our dedication to antisocial cats. We had not been able to save Mitt, and now Jimmy, too, our original cat terrorist, also descended into destruction. The older he got, the more difficult he got, to the point where he, too, had to be quarantined.

Chips, as always, stepped up.

We had a lake house in Minneapolis where we would go for the summer, and in which Chips had an office. It was there that Jimmy was banished; we couldn't let him out.

The office was an unlikely landscape for superheroism, tucked as it was behind all the domestic grind, the kitchen-sink clamor, ever-churning Maytag, and litter box burials and excavation. Though Chips had a major-league mind, the room reflected his T-ball tastes. It was filled with goofy gewgaws, those shiny, showy, worthless trinkets, as well as greeting cards too tender to toss and goodbye-to-the-good-stuff furniture long ago wrecked by our weaponized collection of kitty claws. For Chips, it was work and home. He'd fled the skyscrapers full of edgy art and outrageous overhead of Dallas, and now, thanks to technology like (gasp!) fax machines, Chips could find himself in any sunny corner he wished and still perform his lawyerly magic.

His newfound freedom from anticat office policies (his colleagues both in Dallas and Mayberry frowned upon furry miscreants roaming their hallowed halls, go figure), Chips could indulge in my excited notion of small-fry secretarial help. You know, the kind with pointy ears and four paws. Of course, Chips probably envisioned a soft-hearted marshmallow like Miss Bunny, melting unobtrusively over her favorite lap. Instead, he got the devil himself. Jimmy, our little Antichrist, was propelled into the prestigious office-cat position by none other than our own public-health protective order. For the sake of us and our cat-filled household, Jimmy would be incarcerated in the office. He did not take kindly to his imprisonment. Chips, my hero, became Jimmy's prime target for his feisty, venomous volatility. Through crumpled contracts and decisive, growling oral arguments, Jimmy took up his last stand. Our ancient scrapper, once a beast to behold, was now a fuzzy raisin on four toothpicks, but that did not stop him from attitude to the end. And the whole while, until Jimmy's passing, Chips's affection remained undiluted. Jimmy may have made Oscar the Grouch look like a shaggy green Donny Osmond, but in the end, he was, and would always be, *our* little monster.

One line. There was one line related to math, an analogy of a formula to explain the complex equation of taking in hard-ass rescue cats that end up causing mayhem, destruction, and heartbreak. The story was, as I cognitively suspected, ***not*** about calculus, and where, in those pages about terror-cats and happy-kitty pills, was there any room for my own insecurities? After reading the story, did I still think Betsy might have been too different from me? That she excelled where I had failed? That she, a smart, confident, bighearted person would have still befriended me, a woman stripped bare by a single word in a title about catching cats?

Yes, I determined. Yes, because I could forgive Betsy for her use of the ***calculus*** word. Yes, because she would have laughed at my existential crisis over a humorous line. Yes, because she was generous like that. But more, because she was practical. She'd done everything she could to save Mitt, both from his hardscrabble alley life and from himself and his destructive tendencies, yet ultimately, she understood the reality of the situation. No matter how much she wished for a happy ending, one was not in the cards for Mitt. She had to protect her brood; she had to protect herself. She was feline Florence Nightingale, but she was also realistic. She knew she would have to make the tough decisions—and she did, no matter her own heartbreak. As she said when Jimmy, their other terrorist cat, died, he was ***their*** little monster. No matter what she'd had to do, Betsy still overflowed with empathy.

Which meant she would have listened to my irrational reaction to her choice of title, laughed at my long-winded explanation, then nodded appreciatively.

Practical, analytical—two traits she and I may not have shared—but warm and empathetic—two that we did. It made me feel better, like our rocky relationship had righted itself. It's funny, to think of my time with Betsy's pages as my time with Betsy, as though we had, indeed, lived through opening up to each other, exposing our vulnerabilities. But Betsy ***did*** do that for me. She showed me, in her willingness to do what she had to, how she could hurt from her own life choices. I had cringed at decades-old thoughts of my own "failures"; Betsy had faced her realities head-on, without apology. We ***were*** sharing ourselves.

The written word. Yeah, it's powerful.

Because I'd gotten all that from a single word: *calculus*.

(Okay, still, I shudder at it!)

Chapter 13

Betsy had a rescue cat originally named Skipper by her nieces, who'd found the cat, but she quickly changed his name ("Sorry, girls, but re-titling is always a purr-ogative") to Atticus Finch. Like the word *calculus* in her previous story title, this name, too, hit me with an instantaneous reaction. In this case, though, it was joy. Wide-smile, *Oh yeah, I like her*, comfort. And, like with *calculus*, I was aware the story wouldn't center on the famous literary character Atticus Finch, from Harper Lee's Pulitzer Prize–winning novel *To Kill a Mockingbird*. But that Betsy had named a cat—and not just named, but *changed* his name to—Atticus Finch was all I needed to know. We *were* kindred spirits, after all.

But it wasn't familiarity with the literary character alone that drew me to make another connection with Betsy. It was, like this story, the making of, that also intrigued me. Because from Harper Lee, I learned not just about characterization and writing style and race and culture and American history but also about the writing process itself.

I first encountered Atticus Finch, like many students, in high school. I read *To Kill a Mockingbird* in grade 9 English and loved the story immediately. (Yes, I was one of those kids who actually read the texts in English class. My husband, who'd attended the same high school as me, was not. He assured me it was possible to do just fine ***without*** reading the books—he was proof, he said—but then, he's also an engineer and didn't actually remember who Atticus Finch was, so, maybe not.) I adored Scout, the protagonist who is six at the start of the story and who learns some hard lessons about racism in her hardscrabble Depression-era hometown of Maycomb, Alabama, when Mayella, a poor, abused white girl accuses a Black man of rape. Scout's father, Atticus, is assigned to defend Tom Robinson, and Atticus pours his every effort into the case, to the townspeople's increasingly dangerous dismay. Scout calls her father "Atticus" and assumes every dad is like him. She comes to see that he is, in fact, exceptional as she confronts her growing awareness of despicable injustice in her burgeoning world.

I would go on to teach the book myself as a high school English teacher for many, many years. I have lost count of how many times I've read it. I loved teaching it because it wasn't just about literature. It was about our values.

And our own biases, too. Over time, the book became a source of controversy in the classroom. While still beloved, it also became problematic. How could we continue to teach about race and culture and history using only a book about Black people written by a white woman and centered on a white protagonist? I appreciated the need to address our (mostly white teaching staff's) unconscious bias, though by this time, I had also been teaching books by Black authors for a lot of years.

Still, the questions, while uncomfortable, were essential to our own growth. Could I still love a book written in a different time, about a different time, even with its limitations? Would I, say, name a cat Atticus Finch, with all the focus on the characters' place in our education system?

Yes, yes I would. Because Atticus Finch, through Scout's eyes, is a marvel of a character. Perfect, almost. A dad everyone would want, even with his flaws.

And that is where I encountered the second part of my appreciation for *To Kill a Mockingbird*. The writing process. Atticus *did* come across, many critics argued, as almost too perfect. But in 2015, a year before her death, Harper Lee published her second novel, *Go Set a Watchman*. To great controversy. It turned out that the novel was, in fact, a first draft of *To Kill a Mockingbird* but was presented as a sequel, since it dealt with Scout's perspective as an adult trying to better understand and appreciate her father, whom she had once idolized but was now appearing more bigoted in ways she found shocking. Kind of like us, the readers of the original novel. Lee's initial publisher back in the late 1950s, upon reading this draft, felt it held promise but didn't believe it was ready for publication. Lee then revised the story (and revised and revised), finally resulting in the bestseller we know and love today.

I was as eager as the next fan to pick up *Go Set a Watchman*, despite mixed reviews. After all, we were talking about a Pulitzer Prize–winning author who had never published another novel!

Oh my goodness, the critics were right. It was terrible. Slow pace, underdeveloped characters, clunky dialogue. It was a disappointment.

Until I remembered *it was a first draft!* Oh wow, this was revelatory for me. Here we got to see, in black-and-white, a top author's first efforts. It's easy for readers to assume that what appears in their hands simply flowed, effortlessly, from the fingertips of the author. As a writer, my own experience was nowhere close. I had draft after draft after (horrid) draft of my novels to show my writing process was anything but effortless. Yet here was proof that even the most revered literary icons "stumbled" on their first try.

Only, I also realized, Harper Lee had not "stumbled." Yes, the book as it was published wasn't great. ***But it was a first draft!*** It was never meant to be published—it's why Lee's editor requested revisions in the first place. It made me realize that we, as writers, often completely misjudge a first draft. We say it's terrible, or it's crap, or it's a sodden mess (or other words unfit for general publication), but that's only because we're comparing our first drafts to what we think the final product should be. Of course it's gonna suck! We're measuring our first draft against the wrong criteria. Instead, we need to reframe our criteria. A first draft's *only* purpose is to get ideas out of a writer's head and onto the page. There doesn't have to be good character development or sharp dialogue or strong pacing. There only has to be words on the page. Everything else can come in revisions. Like ***Go Set a Watchman*** turning into *To Kill a Mockingbird*.

Which is what I had in front of me with Betsy's stories. I had a draft, stories not yet ready for publication, a collection of anecdotes that needed editing. I read quotes from Lee's editor Tay Hohoff, who explained there were many hours of discussions with her and Lee as they hammered out revisions.

With Betsy's death, I had no such possibility, but I had a reminder of what a first draft is supposed to be: ideas on page. Full stop. And Betsy's charm, voice, and style already abundantly clear on the page, I was buoyed by the opportunity in front of me. I was excited to meet Betsy's Atticus Finch.

Atticus Finch

Atticus Finch turned up one overbooked Turkey Day (as troublemakers tend to do) in the arms of our bean-sprout nieces Elizabeth and Liv, both full of that wide-eyed, eight-year-old wonder not yet muddied with raging hormones and am-I-cool angst.

They'd arrived earlier that afternoon (sans cat) and had loved trailing our furry congregation around every corner. What seemed an excessive collection of alley scraps to the sad-hearted among us morphed into a magical dreamscape of storybook creatures for those with stardust and sugarplums in their eyes, like the girls. Their adventures in Cat Land were curtailed only by the clock-watching world of pesky parents and other ancient relatives, commandeered away for the taking of Christmas-card photos and elbows-*off*-the-table-and-*please*-pass-the-gravy manner minding.

After dinner and our gastronomic excesses, a good number of relatives, including our nieces, went for a walk. I stayed with my sanity-preserving sous-chef/mother to clean up the carnage, while all others departed en masse to stroll Mayberry's sleepy streets. An hour later, when we weary kitchen fairies finally had our feet up, our horde returned: with an unexpected dinner guest.

Skipper, as they called the poor little darling, was a deliriously cooperative cat. He stuck, snug like Velcro, around the girls' competing arms, shoulders, and necks, as they launched into a tale of their lucky find (though their elders gave a less romanticized version of events). A sweet peep along their path startled the lot of them, and they'd given pause to look up, where they spotted a lonely ball of fluff crouched in the limbs of a boulevard dogwood. It was the eye contact that did it. One look from cat to kids and the precious (pesky) little puss scrambled down to join his dear new valentines (victims). He shadowed his new kid-sized allies until the elders scoured the surrounding trees for a family tree. But a final inspection of ground zero revealed no family ties. Yippee! (Yikes!) The adorable (ignorable) newly named Skipper was scooped up and presented to Auntie Bets, the noted expert (and mad as a hatter) on all cat matters. There were deliberations. I, being a pseudo-optimist (and being over-crittered) urged one last return to the scene of the kit-napping, suggesting a quick deposit and a quicker departure. Surely some distraught cat-daddy was frantically searching for his tree-hugging kitty. On the other side, the smaller (but righteous) We-Love-Skipper-and-Want-to-Take-Him-Home-with-Us contingent declared that idea ludicrous.

"Skipper wouldn't have run away with them if he'd had a happy home life," they argued.

It was hard to disagree, and so, appeasement was the policy of choice. The situation, I conceded, warranted a wait-and-see decree. Skipper (ahem, Atticus Finch, thank you very much) could camp in one of our spare-Fluffy spaces until we found his home. I endeavored to reassure the newest junior members of my game warden team that if we didn't find it, Skipper (ahem, Atticus Finch) would remain in good hands. This was also to reassure the worried parents that they wouldn't be leaving with another furry mouth to feed. Most of the crew were more or less placated, but there were two mighty glum faces when it came time for goodbyes. Poor Elizabeth was almost inconsolable as she kept pleading her case. *Please, please, pleeeeaaasse?* She seemed tempted to simply tuck the tiny creature into their eight-passenger van (Mommy's cat allergies not even a blip on her kitty-crush radar). Liv was no less lovestruck, full of crestfallen sighs as she smothered Skipper with smooches. She was begrudgingly resigned to a melancholy farewell.

And so, the rescue-cat cycle repeated. Skipper's young heroines had accurately assessed his friendless state; my ad returned to the paper, and my favorite repeat customers resurfaced. They'd already taken (and spoiled) a matching father-son mouser set, fueling a hankering for one more debonair cat in their house. I was gleeful as I forwarded the fabulous news to Elizabeth and Liv—only to be met with mediocre *oh-goody* grunts. I sighed. I guess even Fluffy Love fades fast in the single-digit years when the object of one's affection cannot stick around.

It was now December, but there were sad tidings among our Christmas cheer. My father suddenly died. None of us expected his premature passing, but it made us ever more grateful for our last gathering a few weeks earlier at Thanksgiving. The story of Skipper's rescue, therefore, became enmeshed in the heartfelt memories of our last times together.

By January, though, Skipper was back. I'd gotten a distressed call early in the New Year from his new human about the cat's high crimes. In some turf battle with the already-tenured cats, Skipper was trying to stake his own top-dog (uh, cat) status in a dastardly—and decidedly counterproductive—maneuver. He wet his mistress's mattress with a nightly bedtime bladder bomb. All timeouts and triple-washed fresh starts had failed to curb that mess-making. Having run out of ideas and sheets, Skipper's new family reluctantly returned the unrepentant plumbing problem to Pauly boot camp.

And so returned, into the guest bathroom Skipper went. Monkish sequestration was the tried-and-true cure for his bed-wetting—all soakable accessories stowed—and there he could reflect upon the error of his incontinent ways.

Of course, I took him to the vet to rule out any non-naughty root of those urological evils—which we did—only to be broadsided with the revelation that my little devil had a dangerously enlarged heart. My vet, my very own Dr. Dolittle, handed me a stethoscope and offered me a listen. (Harder than it seems with Skipper the super-squirmer. Picture a game of pin the tail on the ticklish donkey.) Instead of a brisk drumbeat, I heard a groggy gurgle, and my own heart clenched. Dr. Dolittle couldn't (or kindly wouldn't) quantify Skipper's odds at getting to gray whiskers. His only prescription was a baby aspirin every few days. With this discovery, Skipper's fate was sealed. I could not (and would not) adopt out a cat with a tired ticker. He would therefore live the remainder of his short-straw life at the Pauly Pet Sanatorium. And in which he would get a new name. If he was going to be staying with me, I would claim my prerogative to rename him Atticus Finch, for my literary hero.

Since there was no more rascally bladder recidivism, I placed my stricken boy with firmly entrenched fellow boarders Mitt and Gretel with the hopes of cheering him through his final few low-battery prowls. It worked. Atticus found a kindred spirit (or like-minded man of monkey business) in Mitt, the barroom brawler turned teddy bear, though Gretel, who was chronically disgruntled anyway, wouldn't give either pesky prankster the time of day. Soon, Atticus had settled right in.

And can you believe it? In contradiction to the fortified pessimism about his chances of living to a ripe old age, Mr. Finch celebrated a decade of autumn anniversaries in our home. He became a good-humored goofball, barking out infectious falsetto laughs, and was universally popular among both his own kind and us humans, the lesser beings. Very rarely did Atticus Finch resort to protest peeing, the behavior that had landed him back in my lap in the first place. Instead, the little clown managed to always worm his charming way into center stage, superglued to preheated laps or wrapped snug around my head while I slept, like he was the latest Cat-*Is*-the-Hat fashion accessory. In one of fate's countless fickle-fingered twists, Atticus outlived many other fallen friends, cheerfully keeping pace with the pouncing pack.

And so it is that late each November, I would think of that long-past Thanksgiving, the last one with my dad, and the first one with a cat, who, by most reckoning, had been a tossed-away table scrap. Two small girls thought otherwise, and I treasured the memory of their wonderfully wide-open hearts—and that wiggling, giggling little critter they left behind.

There's an element of trust thrust onto a reader of an incomplete manuscript. Where we would normally want clarification from the author, in Betsy's case, that was obviously impossible. Had she and I been working together, I would have pressed Betsy to tell me more about her dad's passing. *How did you feel?* I would say. *How close were you? What kind of relationship did you have with him? How did he die? How did you cope?* Because, wouldn't you agree, that the sudden death of a beloved parent would trump the adoption of a literally heart-sick cat? And so I would have shifted Betsy's narrative, from the story about her cat Atticus Finch to the story about, well, *her*.

But no doubt your father's death had an incredible impact on your life, I could hear myself arguing with Betsy.

Yes, of course, she'd reply. I imagine a huff in her voice, as though the statement were obvious (it was). *But so did Atticus Finch*.

And *that* is what I would have missed had I been focused getting Betsy to turn her story inward. I would have missed the profound effect a beloved animal can have; I would have downplayed the gentle, daily joy of more than a decade of love this tiny creature gave to Betsy in favor of the dramatic, heart-wrenching death of her father. That is not to say his death meant nothing to Betsy; it is only to say that *this* story wasn't *that* story. This story was about two young girls who found a cat, who had to leave a cat, and who placed the cat into their aunt's warm and capable hands. They gave Betsy their trust (albeit reluctantly, given their pleas to keep him), and Betsy rewarded that trust.

In *To Kill a Mockingbird*, Harper Lee introduces us to Scout's neighbor, Mrs. Dubose, a mean, racist, sexist old lady, always angry and badmouthing Scout and her older brother, Jem. One day Jem loses his temper at her name-calling and cuts off all the heads of her camellia flowers. As punishment, he is forced by Atticus to go read to her. Scout accompanies him, and they witness Mrs. Dubose sick and dying. After she passes away, Atticus explains that she'd become addicted to the morphine she'd been taking for her pain and wanted to rid herself of her dependency before she died. Jem and Scout's presence was a distraction as she rode out her withdrawal symptoms.

At first Mrs. Dubose's storyline seems an unlikely tangent for Scout's story—she's obsessed with the case against Tom Robinson, like the rest of the town—but Scout learns a valuable lesson about courage. Harper Lee shows us, as a parallel to Atticus's own struggle about doing what's right in the face of great obstacles, that Mrs. Dubose did not choose the easy way out. She could have taken the pain medication to ease herself into death, but she chose instead to fight to uphold her own moral code—that she would be beholden to nothing in the last days of her life.

Betsy's charming story about Atticus Finch (the cat) shows us a similar quiet parallel. In this tale, we learn of heartbreak and tragedy in the death of her father, yet Betsy still chooses to shine her light on the joys of taking in and caring for a heart-sore, goofball cat. It's not all about the big drama in our lives but about the small, heartfelt moments, too.

So perhaps I was wrong about first drafts after all. Perhaps Betsy did have a lot more to share before an editor like me could "fix" things. Perhaps we do sometimes need to stop and take a minute to read what first comes out on the page. It is, indeed, the truest way to show us an author's true heart on their sleeve.

Chapter 14

No person (or cat) is an island. It takes a village . . . we are not alone. Betsy may have been a spectacular driving force in her determination and dedication to animal welfare, but she was quick to recognize she was not in this business alone. In her writing, she had put together vignettes of people she'd met, friends and neighbors, who'd shared her joy in pets. In them, she was as enthralled with the humans of the story as much as the cats. She recognized kindred spirits and took pleasure in their pleasure. And challenges. And frustrations. Because, yes, cats especially can make you want to tear your hair out.

As I read Betsy's assorted snippets, I thought of my own friends and neighbors, especially those with whom I had bonded over our pets. Some have dogs, and others, like me, have too many cats. And no matter the animal makeup, we still managed to spend hours swapping stories, bemoaning vet bills, and commiserating in the critterly hijinks that rule most of our lives.

Pets are connection, not just with the humans in their household but a commonality in which we can all indulge.

I liked that Betsy included her human friends in her writing with as much good-hearted humor as she wrote about the animals. She was not, as Chips explained, an insular, soapbox-spewing fanatic.

"Betsy always had an expression," Chips said. "'Nobody likes a zealot.' She tried not to wear her animal welfare on her sleeve. She would never lecture people on animals or what she saw at Walmart or how bad people could be. She was aware she had to almost compartmentalize that part of her. Everybody knew she was kind to the animals and that we had animals and that we'd take them in and she'd have interesting stories, but she wasn't perceived as an animal nut."

It takes restraint to stand your ground, stick to your principles, but also have the good grace to appreciate the importance of social interactions. Betsy had a message; Betsy spoke her mind, but Betsy also knew her way around people as much as animals.

And, as we all know, people aren't easy.

Saint Beatriz

Weaned on Lake Wobegon's flannel-shirt-and-Chevrolet ways, I'm ashamed to admit to a streak of flashy excess. But Chips and I are, in fact, a couple of addicts when it comes to real estate. We're a grab-the-checkbook kind of people when cool property gets dangled before our dilated eyes. We salivate at the slightest MLS provocation, always on the prowl for the next mortgageable morsel lurking around any corner.

But what kind of real-estate craving could have possibly propelled our Brazilian friends Beatriz and Gonzalo from uprooting their lives in Ipanema paradise to come to our pioneer-prairie hamlet? The delectable fruit of the Federal Reserve, it turned out, and Gonzalo's career quest for greenback gold.

That, however, left poor Bea and her samba-filled soul adrift. With an empty day planner and an idle heart, Bea found her way to a local pet repository, the inaugural site of our sisterhood. She was a fellow four-paw fanatic, and here she found her true calling. Among the woeful droves of best (furry) friends, Bea managed to single-handedly drag that dismal dog dump into the current century.

Not everyone was impressed. The mutiny spearheaded by Bea, a feisty foreigner, was met with no small share of bristling backsides from the established denizens. Bea, with her speed-speak, arm-waving, and hair-trigger temper, was a force to be reckoned with. But Bea wielded motives as pure as puppy love, even if there was no pussyfooting around with her. Saint Beatriz charged ahead in her epic underdog overhaul of the shelter. She would even foster wayward cats in her garage and scrape together a war chest penny by penny. She was a kind, whole-hearted soul, but yes, also an unchained pit bull who persevered through brick walls and other challenging people. Yes, she strained her husband, bank balance and nerves, but she was steadfast in her crusade for every down-and-out little wet nose.

But the fight was real. The commitment you have to take on to protect the animals is enormous. The people active in animal welfare, even those who run a small shelter in small communities, are dedicated, yes, but they're not always business people, not always practical, and may not always understand how things need to work in an organization. This leads to infighting and personality conflicts. It was into this structure that Bea, my dearest ally in alley matters, appeared, and out of this structure that Bea finally chose to leave. Her inner armor had worn thin; selfless altruism can carry a heavy price, but it was one my heroic friend paid without hesitation. The countless little lives she tenderly shepherded were living proof.

Furry Tales

There is a *cat*alog of never-say-never tales, especially when it comes to cat-haters turned cream puffs who have fallen under the spell of some wayward little bit of fluff. There is such folly in "No Fluffy!" proclamations, as our good friends Barbara and Mike discovered. The Texas twosome were gaga for each other and their idyllic look-but-don't-touch fiefdom. They lived in a perpetual *House & Garden* photo spread. Their home would befit a backdrop for any queen bee of high-brow homeowners from coast to coast. (Oh, how her shades of blue blood must have curdled slumming it among our dorm-room-for-furry-dropout design scheme!) The prospect of inserting one of those purring critters into Barbara's hermetically sealed haven seemed impossible. I just couldn't picture those perfectly lacquered fingers sullied by a litter box, nor could I imagine her witnessing a cat heaving hairballs onto her expensive sofa. Perish the thought of cat claws upon the same. Barbara offered polite interest in our menagerie, but at no time did my dear friend indicate any inkling or aspiration toward cat ownership.

But will wonders never cease . . . one day I got a voicemail from Mr. and Mrs. Clean, hinting at some giddy discovery during an unlikely country outing. I had to laugh at the idea of their Green Acres daytrip, the two of them meandering along dusty farm roads in their shiny bigshot-mobile. I wasn't sure what they could have discovered, to be honest. Since Barbara's top-dollar tastes run modern, I ruled out any rusty antiquities. Perhaps some mouthwatering mason-jar memento?

I must admit to a healthy verbosity, but oh my speechless surprise when we visited their garage! Nowhere was there some prize-winning pickle relish. Instead, the garage had been scrubbed to brain-surgery standards, and in it, curled up in a tastefully appointed cardboard crib, was a runty little bit of a kitten. I stared at her in wide-eyed wonderment; the kitten stared back, equally mesmerized.

"Oh, she was in such a pathetic state!" Barbara exclaimed as she fussed and fawned, prattling on about the little kitten's rescue. When they'd found her languishing, they decided immediate action was necessary.

I couldn't contain a wry smile. Barbara and Mike had often quirked their skeptical smirks at my own roundup stories, but now I could welcome the spic-and-span couple into our ranks of surplus critter collectors.

This was, indeed, a Cinderella story, and there surely was never a young maiden, whiskered or otherwise, who had a more meteoric rags-to-riches tale. Prissy Missy Kitty Kat went from hay bales to *Architectural Digest* in one fell swoop. She moved into supersanitized Cadillac quarters, a.k.a. the Prissy Palace; she bonded atop her benefactors' laps during their daily poolside siesta; she had the best veterinary care her sugar daddy and mama could buy. Naturally, Barbara assured us, the kitten would stay in the garage; her house's halls were hallowed, of course. But just as naturally as falling in love, those best-laid game plans went out the window.

"Well, it was a tad chilly out there at night," Barbara admitted a few days later, less to my shock and awe than to my mirthful chuckle. "She's in the laundry room." Finally, we were told, to no great surprise, that their dear girl had been given license to roam the entire exquisite square footage at will. Picture a pint-sized calico with a crooked little smile pussyfooting through her obstacle course of objet d'art, sunbathing on a preheated Persian carpet, or disappearing into a downy bazillion-thread-count cat bed.

What's even more amusing (to me, at least) was that Prissy's two puny pounds of fur burst open the floodgates, paving the way for a steady parade of other little pip-squeaks mysteriously turning up at Hacienda de Hairball Highlife. Having stumbled upon the path of Kitty-Ritz hospitality, our pals kept rolling out the red carpet for every downtrodden puss that prowled their white-gloved way.

Ultimately, Prissy's biography is a favorite fairy tale, a head-shaking, smile-making reminder of all the unpredictably happy four-pawed possibilities in life.

Surplus-Puss Superhero

Our buddy Bill was another example of a heart weakened by—no, *strengthened* by—pussycat pressure. He, bless his heart, epitomized the slippery slope of "just one more . . ."

Of course, neighborly compatibility is always hit or miss. But in Bill's case, we hit the jackpot in our critters-come-first, free-spirited next-door neighbor. Long ago lured far from

Main Street by the tropical margaritas-and-senoritas slow lane, Bill the bachelor returned to his native Smallville in deference to the last wishes of his mother, in her mid-eighties. Apparently, someone forgot to tell the woman she wasn't actually nearing her expiration date, because more than a decade later, sixty-year-old Bill was still keeping house for his spry centenarian. (She lived until she was 102!) Faithfully, Bill catered to her whimsical wants, shielding Mayberry's grandest dame from every peccadillo beyond her doorstop. Oh, she was a domineering woman. Picture a gray-haired son wolfing down an entire pecan pie in his garage—with the clandestine fervor of a CIA operative—so as not to upset his mama's strict dietary dictates. I recall a story Chips told of a time the two of them returned from a fishing trip and Chips offered him a remaining six-pack of beer.

"No! Put that back in your car! My mother doesn't allow me to drink!"

Such was the big heart of a man who took care of others. He was also a man who paid no heed to the dollar-and-daily-grind lifestyle, having returned to his mother's house without a job lined up, and all the happier for it.

But I do profess that my barely constrained cat-hoarding habit must have rubbed off on Bill—and then some. It happened, no doubt, after one of the many times he would cat sit for us when we were away. Infected by me with cat fever, once Bill got started with his first cat, his own menagerie mushroomed. He never had to look far for a whiskery waif to be salvaged. Most any trip to Mayberry's Walmart would find a cardboard box full of FREE little Fluffys and Fidos, where some dope would haphazardly pass them out to any willing taker—responsible-pet-owner material or not. I confess I was not a fan of the store, a scourge of small-town enterprise, but I became even more enraged when the management disinclined to act upon some nutty blonde's repeated rantings over a few batches of fleabags. I would try to preach my furry-family-planning pitch directly to the culprits who'd allowed such wanted procreation to happen in the first place, and I would try to use as much diplomacy as I, a bare-fanged Virgo, could muster. Finally, I would resort to offering cold, hard cash for them to spay or neuter the animals, thus closing the complimentary furball factory.

Dear Bill, on the other hand, did not preach. He was already a convert and was unable to pass by one of those Bud Light boxes of leftover babies-to-go without lightening the load by at least one. I could not tell you how many cats Bill looked after at the height of his insanity (after he'd bought a five-acre parcel of land and fenced it in), but it was upward of one hundred.

When he was owner of but four cats, he put a big stake in the middle of the backyard. In the evenings, he'd bring these four cats out on leashes, and he'd connect them to the stake so they could walk around. It was like a compass as they went in four different directions! Bill was not satisfied, no, not in the least, so he'd also built a contraption, or a kennel, I suppose, though to be honest, carpentry was not Bill's strong suit. In his bedroom, off his window, he'd built a cage of chicken wire, allowing the cats a chance at fresh outdoor air. And his obsession grew. After his mother passed, he had a screened-in structure built, complete with pond water flowing in the middle. Inside was shelving for the cats, by this time numbering in the dozens. He installed a fence because, by all rights (and town codes), he could have no more than three cats. The fence would hide his upward of thirty.

Yet I assure you, there is no hiding thirty-plus cats. The odor was tremendous, and though I could appreciate Bill's soft spot for the cats, many other neighbors could not live with the consequences. With a squirming snarl of constant cat confusion barely keeping nosy neighbors and the long arm of the law at bay, Bill bought a new parcel of land outside of town. He had this property fenced, too, with special top-of-the-line chain link so the cats could not climb out. He was conscientious, too. He'd designed different "zones" for the cats: one zone held kitties with feline leukemia, so they could not infect the others; another was for cats with feline AIDS; and there were some zones in which none could cross, in order to protect them all. Bill had a big storage building brought onto the property and insulated igloos set up all for the winter. He would bring in three hundred pounds of cat food—the good stuff, too, nothing cheap—and he would bring in his tender heart and tender care.

If that wasn't a surplus-puss superhero, I didn't know what was. Fussing over his four-legged family just as obligingly as he was mollycoddled by his mama, Bill lived above the fickle-hearted fray, all for fur, all the time.

Cat Charmers

Wendy, my never-a-false-step friend, was a cat person to her husband Don's all-dog-all-the-time person. She was tea and crumpets to his Bud and buddies. Together they were a real-life Lady-and-the-Tramp mismatch made in heaven. And, as Wendy favored felines and Don favored Wendy, so it was that they had cats.

But their first furry batch had already gone to the great catnap in the sky by the time Chips and I and our wall-to-wall assortment of furry critters arrived. So when we met, they were catless.

"I must meet your dirty dozen!" Wendy cried.

"There may be a *head-for-the-hills* stampede among the hermits at the first hint of a foreign invasion," I warned.

Wendy waved me off, and then all 101 tiny pounds of her dropped down to the floor, cooing, "Here, kitty, kitty, kitty," to the invisible gang. And just as I was putting my jaw back in place, out of the woodwork tiptoed every last bashful cat, going nose to nose with Wendy the Cat Charmer. I was dumbstruck! After all those years wading in ankle-high anarchy, why hadn't *I* come up with that neat little trick? And then a slow, beaming smile stretched my face, my gratitude for the friendship gods who planted me within shouting distance of an equally untethered Crazy Cat Lady. We four heads-of-furry-households hit it off from the get-go. My *cat*titude had always been "love me, love my critters"; Wendy met my requirement in spades, cementing our budding sisterhood for all time.

In a bucket list of life's best-ofs, there really aren't any finer hours than the irresistible combination of bosom buddies and big laughs. Don raised the good-times bar to a whole new level; he could have us all, with the slightest snickering provocation, spontaneously combust into the kind of hysterical hootenanny that makes you howl just thinking about it. A borrowed wrench somehow turns into a borrowed beer, and then another, and then forget that stinking leak, the Grand Poobah of play-now-plumb-later has led you down the Pabst Blue Ribbon path once again.

But among all that merrymaking was one glaring omission. A cat. No matter my beseeching pleas, which were met with assenting nods and wistful sighs, Wendy and Don did not get a cat. Then, just as I'd given up the idea of squeezing a needy little newcomer into Mr. and Mrs. Energizer Bunny's fast lane of fun, we were whisked over to their house.

To meet their out-of-the-blue bouncing bundle of kitty joy.

Zipper the Zany, two pounds of high-octane *zoom*, made even his whirling-dervish cat-daddy's head spin. Zip was a locomotion in motion, flying a whole lot higher and living a whole lot larger than the average ball of fluff. Naturally, only the crème de la crème of house-creature comforts would do for their new kitten—not just any old carpet-scrap-and-two-by-four tiny-tiger tree for Zip, no, but a designer forest of high-pile Frasier firs. Forget disposable Dixie (upon which the dishwasher at Chez Pauly Chats insists), we're talking crystal kibble service. Of course, it came with the haute-est cuisine and cosmic catnip money could buy. Auntie Betsy was now routinely shamed by her own bourgeois feline furnishings and the passé culinary qualifications of her (cringing-Cadillac-priced) livestock feed.

Soon enough, a second sprout was fished from the local down-and-out stockpile (there ought to be a surgeon general's warning outside those Costco-O'-Cats doors: *Caution*: Contents Highly Addictive). Crowned Cleopatra, the kitty arrived, much to Zipper the Spoiled's *you-have-*got*-to-be-kidding* chagrin, and rounded out the fur family to *purr*fection.

And then, along came an unbearable reminder that even the most magical of minutes and days only move in one direction. In this life, there are no time-outs. No do-overs.

Just, tick-tock, tick-tock . . .

Plane crash . . .

Tick-tock, tick-tock . . .

Died on impact . . .

Don was gone.

Our wild and crazy, live-out-loud, once-in-a-blue-moon friend was gone.

Don's larger-than-life life, had, in fact, turned out to be as fragile and fleeting as the rest of ours.

Wendy somehow kept going, putting one foot in front of the other, juggling the monumental life debris of the disastrously departed. But no creature was as brokenhearted as Zipper. All the little cat's *zoom* disappeared as he fell into a serious slump by the inexplicable (to a cat) disappearance of his hung-the-moon human, awaiting a happy human homecoming that will never be.

Even the very luckiest—and I am at the tip-top of that pink-cloud list, with a life as charmed as they come—can count our true friends on precious few fingers. Those rare bosom buddies see us through the rosiest of glasses. And while it is easy to find our true four-legged friends (just a shelter stop away, always loving even the least lovable among us), it is nearly impossible to collect and hold close the heaven-sent hugs and kisses from our fellow humans. Chips and I, like poor Zip, were beyond fortunate to be a part of Don's life, even if only for a while.

Art's Passion

Chips's long tenure in the Lone Star State bestowed him—and by happy association, his Yankee bride—a fill of fabulous friends. Among all the line-dancing BBQ-and-beer buddies, dearest Arthur shined with superlatives from all angles. Among *his* fortunate inner circle is one big-haired, bigger-hearted mama, a deliciously eccentric ensemble of family-by-choice, and Jackson. Jackson, at first blush, seemed to be just a run-of-the-meow-mill tabby, but it turned out he was that rarely recorded freak of nature: the militantly obedient mouser.

Art and Jackson were a most fortuitous pairing. Art was passionately devoted to his home and his plethora of objets d'art, which consisted of anything and everything from primitive homespun to pricey highbrow, prehistoric to post-modern, miniature to mammoth, mainstream mementos to mighty strange stuff (just a sampling: 187 crystal decanters, 23 elephantine étagères crammed full of groves of fancy gewgaws, Ming urns, and an adorable deceased Yorkie under glass). The place demanded white-glove fastidiousness right down to the household's furry inhabitant. Jackson, shockingly, could actually comply. He obliged his persnickety human with cotillion courtesies.

Let me assure you, Jackson's conformity to law and order was indeed incongruous among cats, and it did raise in my mind broader philosophical questions. Is the helter-skelter world of housecats, who pride themselves on being first-class contrarians and avid anarchists, just waiting for some properly pitched rules and regulations? Have we prematurely thrown in the tabby-training towel? Do we renege on honing any good habits in cats in favor of their canine consorts, who will do anything for kibble and kisses? Art would say yes, and then he would support his argument with the incontrovertible evidence of one ship-shape, long-tailed lieutenant.

Such was not, surely, my own experience with the ragtag Pauly platoon. No, our hooligans were adept at succumbing to tantalizing temptations. No décor in our house was safe from kitty vandalism. Yet Jackson had somehow learned to subdue his *cat*titude, dutifully foregoing all such escapades under Art's watchful eye. Even when Art was in his corner-office day job, Jackson would easily prowl their sardine-packed palace in search of sun, snacks, and a nice snooze without a single crash of Art's private-museum-like collection of curiosities. Jackson could weave among the breakable baubles, the acres of art, the tassels, the toiles, the tapestries, the tureens, all without a single shimmering shard of carnage. In fact, Jackson could grace and space with the purring prima donna stage presence of a cat.

I fully credited Art's boot-camp-for-critters tough love.

It was a sight to behold. From any far-flung corner of the house, Jackson could run toward Art's dinnertime call. Yes, my own untrainable cats were always on high alert for food, but Jackson stood head and shoulders above any riffraff. He would approach his bowl and stand stoically at attention, as frozen as the Queen's Guard, awaiting orders. He would simply *wait*, whether Art's commands were seconds or even minutes away.

Only on command would he dive in. (And receive a hearty pat from the boss and astonished cheers from the rest of us in the peanut gallery.) Could *we* train up our little tigers in the same way? Perhaps we hadn't adequately tested our kitties sufficiently. Perhaps we'd been letting them off the hook too easily, veering toward a path of least resistance.

I'm reminded of Hoover, our hide-but-don't-seek Himalayan, who soaked up every silly trick of the canine trade for one measly treat. Surprisingly, he could effortlessly execute Shake, Sit Up, Roll Over, and the ever-popular Play Dead (the Pauly cocktail party pièce de résistance). At the time, we were greenhorn pet parents, so we assumed that the pretty darling was some sort of vaudevillian savant.

It made me wonder, as I considered Jackson's skill and Art's training, whether the rest of our cat couch potatoes were indeed brimming with hidden talents yet too sublime to demonstrate. Were they, I wondered, just coasting through their nine lives on good looks and cheeky charm alone?

Jackson and Art, I am dismayed to say for all those slacker cats out there, had really set the bar too high.

Houdini's Story

Art had experience with exceptional cats before Jackson. He'd taken in Houdini from a former coworker—but this cat had had a vastly different upbringing.

Houdini had been a lab rat. One of millions used and abused in medical and industrial research, unprotected by any Bill of Rights for Fellow Mammals. Houdini lived a horrible life before Art.

It is unclear to me—and yes, I will proudly climb onto my soapbox on this most contentious matter—how any right-minded person could allow such travesties. I grant that we can all marvel at modern medical miracles, but those breathtaking breakthroughs are ethically muddied by the suffering of all those animals. One must have major moral lapses if one can calculate the cruel price paid by these voiceless victims and still think we come out ahead. But still, there are those who argue no one is being cruel. *They do not feel pain, fear, or loneliness as we do.* That is a blatantly asinine assumption, ignorant of the true nature of these creatures, who crave hugs and kisses as much as we do. They're our support structure, ultra intuitive and glued to our sides through blue funks; they comfort us as we comfort them. They are not robots. Why else do you think the scientists *want* to use these living, breathing creatures? Because biologically, they *are* like us! It is utter illogical malarkey to argue they're not like us in the comfort and care that they need yet *are* like us enough so that we can benefit from their torture.

I argue, too, it also the fault of our culture, in which medicine men, often deep in the hip pocket of Big Pharma, have turned a blindly overmedicating eye to the many twists and turns of our mind/body pretzel. We are not cells and tissues alone. Nor are the animals on which they experiment. Now think about the isolated lives the lab animals lead, far removed from their furry social order. These poor pets have no one to show concern or care for them, the way you do with your own feline family member. How is that ethical?

And those who cry truth? Like People for the Ethical Treatment of Animals? They, like all bearers of really bad news, are often treated with a cringe. They are vilified by all who fear scrutiny and frank discourse, yet they deserve full credit for drawing back those wicked curtains. We don't want to look at ugly, but ugly is what they show us.

Okay, if one abhors the mistreatment of lab animals but can concede the value of medical research as imperative to our own health, safety, and survival, how then can one justify the value of cosmetics and cleaning supplies? Do we need a new mascara so badly that we'll risk the lives of the same creatures we'd welcome into our homes as family? But the companies dress up their medieval evil in platitudes of customer care. Of course we want our consumer products to be safe. But at Fluffy's and Fido's expense? Think about that the next time you slab on makeup or spritz out air freshener. Of course, if you can't imagine such inhumanity, then PETA will gladly send you all the nightmarish nonfiction you can stomach. Even a sneak peek by fair-minded folks at these dungeon-worth details is enough to fire up some blue-chip boycotting. Voting with one measly wallet at a time might seem like a drop in the bucket of Big Business, but the drip-drip-drip of dollar upon disillusioned dollar—spent or spurned—has flooded boardrooms with tidal waves of deep PR doo-doo and drowned bottom lines.

For some strange (and, frankly, lamentable) reason, we, in our short-sighted, self-serving society, have subjugated every living thing on this planet to our own whims and desires. But if we stop all the justification for just a minute, that ancient wisdom whispers the right thing to do: just care. Care enough to make sure that every progressive step we master on the backs of our evolutionary underlings has crystal clear *cans* and *cannots* that respect the animals' own humanity. If that sounds contradictory, then all you need to do is imagine your own little Fluffy or Fido BFF behind those loveless bars.

Like Houdini.

Hairy Houdini, through no fault of his own, had spent the prime of his pet-hood stuck in a cramped cage, at the clinical disposal of his keepers (a prison for even the most nimble-pawed of escape artists). That bum rap in solitary confinement had rewired Houdini's Siamese sass into some cross-eyed semblance of Nice Kitty, even after he'd left the Big House. Because he had never experienced the luxury of latitude to go his own persnickety way, nor tasted that pleasure of pounce-at-will within his cage, the middle-aged cat kept to a strict spatial discipline in Art's expansive house. Though Houdini was no longer blocked by bars, he nonetheless honored Art's pride in his home. He had no reason to look before he leapt because he never leapt. Art's treasure-packed upper shelves remained unsullied by fur.

He did not escape unscathed, however. Houdini the parolee continued to howl his concerns. Art didn't know if he was recalling his protests over his past brutality or conversing after long years in lab-limbo—but all that indecipherable racket carried on until he came to Camp Pauly. This was before my time; Chips was then an oh-so-happy-go-lucky bachelor, and though he was a rising, shining legal and social star, he had not, as of then, demonstrated any cat-sitting skills. It was no wonder Art approached him with skepticism. Chips was known to have a revolving door of freewheeling revelers (*mi casa de fiestas es su casa de fiestas*), was known to have clueless caregiving credentials (wasn't that what maids and mothers were for?), and was known to have Old-Brother-Hubbard provisions (milk, mustard, beer) in his kitchen. He was not an obvious choice to play Mary Poppins to a lab-cat rescue. He did, however, like cats, particularly Houdini, so when Art went away on business, Houdini came to stay.

And it was under Chips's freewheeling care that the once-floor-bound kitty was floor-bound no more. Art had insisted that Houdini never climbed on his counters, but one small visit to Uncle Chips, and the floodgates to domestic disobedience were opened.

It was easy! Chips would recount to me years later with gleeful relish. There was, it turned out, little persuasion to lure that darned cat from his hardwood hangout up onto the higher plane of countertops. Chowtime saw both carefree carousers eating at the counter; Houdini's libations came straight from the faucet, and all sorts of hairball hedonism hijinks ensued.

He was a changed cat. By the time Art came home, his stiff, stilted kitty had done a 180 into a tom-about-townhouse. Art was speechless, but Chips just laughed. Obviously, Houdini's anarchy, hardwired into his feline DNA, had been reignited.

Art, with a crazy unbridled cat on his hands, vastly different than the cautious creature he'd left behind, could, in the end, only laugh too.

Cat Mechanics

Who among us hasn't seen the stereotype of big-mouthed mechanics, the sleazy stuff of news exposés and recurring nightmares? But books, covers, you know. With space-age diagnostic dragnets, the industry really *is* rocket science, and tinkering is relegated to late-night reruns and the great analog rust heap. As a customer, therefore, I was a lost little lamb, at the mercy of high-tech, high-skilled mechanics in all matters under the modern hood.

Imagine, then, my gratitude, when Chips and I were taken under the wing of Mayberry's white knight of piston power, a straight-talking mechanical car doctor named Dale.

And imagine, then, my delight to learn that Dale and his family hosted a herd of cats casually employed in the shop, creating all sorts of chaotic clerical high jinks. I could still picture Mrs. D perched precariously on the last inches of a chair otherwise taken over by a shameless loafer sprawled out behind her in a full-figured snoring splendor.

Dale explained the origin of his cat companions. Years earlier, a shadowy sliver of a cat turned up on his welcome mat, a scruffy streetwalker but for a telltale tummy announcing her imminent state of maternity. Without a blink, Dale gave the downtrodden girl a front-office file-clerk gig. A half-dozen mewling bundles of joy arrived in short order. Soon, the bustling beehive of steels and wheels evaporated into hushed reverence for the newborns as a steady stream of well-wishers (and curiosity-seekers) peered through the "pay here" window. I could think only of the delicious sigh of gruff workmen fawning tenderly over tiny kittens and could do nothing but smile at Dale's tale.

The wayward mama had had her fill of the low life; she harbored no inclination to seek out the cold, cruel world beyond the OPEN sign, and that docility carried over to the next generation. Not once did any of the kitties stray beyond the EMPLOYEES ONLY door. But the little interns inevitably grew into full-cat-sized pseudo-staff. And full-cat-sized trouble, too, as they left no stone—and no wastebasket or wiper-blade box—unturned in their chaos of bumper-to-bumper, high-jumper bedlam. Cute as it may have been, alas, it was a place of business, so finally, Mama Cat and her kids were retired to the boss's bed. Only the best litter buddies remained, becoming the mascots of the monkey-wrench business they were born to be.

In high school, my friend's mother approached me. "You're a good influence on Dee," she said.

I wasn't naive; I knew what she meant. I was a "good girl"; I studied hard and worked harder and had not been found at nearly as many bush bashes as Dee (though what my parents didn't know—or Dee's parents didn't know—didn't hurt them). Dee's mom was worried about her daughter (though in hindsight, she had no reason), and she was grateful I was Dee's friend. But at the time, the comment was a mystery to me. It wasn't that I was keeping Dee on the straight and narrow, nor was she corrupting me. Instead, Dee and I just ***got*** each other. We were likeminded people, despite her parents' misplaced worry.

Like attracts like. We gravitate toward people who are like us, in some fundamental way. We may have different interests, different habits, or different lifestyles—after all, our friends are not our doppelgängers—but still, we connect on a level that reassures us our friends ***see*** us.

Betsy found her people. They shared her love of cats, yes, but it was less about their actions and more about their heart.

Each of the friends Betsy described ***got*** her. They shared her heart and her spirit.

Her heart and spirit were also what attracted me to Betsy, as I read her stories. So yes, I felt like ***I*** could be friends with ***her***, but was I not arrogant to assume ***she*** would be friends with ***me***? After all, after death, she had no way of contradicting my claim. ***No, I don't even*** know ***her!*** she could have argued. Was I not taking something from her by suggesting we were friends? By implying a behavior she could never choose for herself?

The danger of co-opted "ownership," if you will, is real, but I ***knew*** that wasn't the case with Betsy. It was as if we were friends—friends on both sides—because like gravitates toward like.

Betsy wasn't afraid to be her full, authentic self.

It's also how I came to see myself.

Chapter 15

It was a gorgeous June evening, the summer I was sixteen. I'd been home for a week after a three-month exchange to France. It should have been the adventure of my life, a grand experience living with a host family in a completely different country, continent, and culture. It wasn't. My billet and I were too different; we had nothing in common, so she ignored me. I was shy and quiet overseas, so I'd had difficulty making friends at my new and strange school. I came from a family with only one sister; in France, I'd lived with a family of six kids, plus me, plus a baby on the way. It was easy for me to get lost in the chaos of the big family, so for three long months, I felt extraordinarily lonely. In those days, long before internet or email, there was only expensive long-distance phone calls, so instead of imposing on my host family, I would sneak away to a public phone booth (they existed back in those days!) and call my parents collect. I tried to make the best of my exile, though of course, everyone around me crowed at my good fortune. But honestly, all I wanted to do was get back to my own life.

That lasted for one week before my parents crushed us all.

It was a Sunday. We were having dinner in the dining room, where we always had dinner on Sundays. It was what formal dining rooms were for. The evening sun, a beautiful butter yellow, streamed in through the open window. The air was light, a soft breeze blowing. We'd finished eating. My dad, at the head of the table, spoke up.

"Girls," he said, his tone grave and solemn, "your mother and I are separating."

There was a pause. If time folds in on itself, it must have then, because I recall a minute of utter silence in which there was no thought, no breath, no life.

Then my eye traveled to the top corner of the room, by the window. It was empty, of course, but I was surprised. Shocked. Not at the announcement, not right away, but because there was no hidden camera. There *must* have been a hidden camera. We must have been on a cruel episode of *Candid Camera*.

That was my only explanation.

Because not *once* in all my sixteen years had my parents fought, argued, cursed, or berated each other. Not once had any agony they might have felt leaked out of their relationship and into the household. Later, in retrospect, I *still* could not find evidence. It wasn't that I had ignored or dismissed evidence of their crumbling relationship—*it hadn't been there*. My sister confirmed my theory but then conceded she'd only become suspicious during my three-month absence. My parents had done an admirable job of keeping their problems to themselves. Problems that, later, they'd explain had been going on for years.

Blindsided could not have begun to explain my pain.

After dinner, the details of which I no longer remember, I fled to my best friend's house. I never needed an invitation, so I walked right in.

"Jen!" Mrs. Ritchie greeted me with her usual, wide mom-smile. "Come join us for dessert. We're celebrating our wedding anniversary."

I almost fainted.

I held it together all through dessert. When I pulled Diane aside and told her my news, she gaped at me. Her mom, having heard from my mom, came in, gently chastising me for putting up with their celebration.

"I didn't want to ruin it for you," I cried.

Diane left and returned with her dog. She was small, black, and yappy and had an unfortunate fur condition that left her nose and ears bald. She was adorable. Diane placed her in my arms, and over this poor puppy being squeezed too hard, I sobbed.

The memory is far from happy, but it was what sprang to mind when I read Betsy's stories that invoked her own family. There is no correlation in plot; Betsy wrote of a pet from her family's history, a wily creature who wormed his way into everyone's heart, and a feel-good story about the adoption of her sister-in-law's new baby, a beloved niece, and how she negotiated with her husband. Her tone, sweet with a bit of sass, matched the rest of her stories; there was no darkness, despair, or divorce. Yet the memory of my own family's demise surged nonetheless, and it took me a good long while to figure out why.

It was the way Betsy wrote about her family, with all the love and exasperation that goes along with the most loving and exasperating of families. It was the opposite of that June night when I was sixteen, the opposite of what I then thought about family. Decades have passed since that horrible dinner; my views on family have shifted and morphed and evolved and changed, and while I, too, can now gleefully recount my family's adventures with the same sweet-sassy tone, I hadn't appreciated until I read Betsy's stories that her tone was exactly what I'd been striving for that day. I hadn't known, at the time, that the way Betsy could talk of her family's pet stories was the way I would ultimately aim to talk about my own family. It was like her stories were a bookend. On one side, that dark, calamitous divorce day; on the other, Betsy's loving attitude of family for which I had unknowingly and unconsciously strived. Reading Betsy's stories reminded me that I had, after all, arrived.

Rough and Ready Bingo

There was a tender tale of a lost-and-found hound from Mother's childhood. It was a tale told and retold, carried forward into the next generation and the one after that.

A century ago there was a dainty lady named Ella Johnson, a woman whose ninety-nine-pound packaging belied a bulwark of wit and tungsten-spined will, who married the boy next door. Edwin Mork was long-limbed and short-winded, a Norwegian, a bachelor and a farmer, who had migrated to Minneapolis, the mecca of new-world Vikings. They would later become my grandparents. The couple would cling reverently to their *ya-sure-you-betcha!* roots as they welcomed a quartet of daughters, who grew into jitterbugs and jive-talk. One of them, baby Bette, fell hard for a big band hepcat. They would later become my parents.

With four daughters and a wife, Ed was pathetically outnumbered. Though he'd traded in his plow for a Pontiac, he still craved the twelve-gauge hunt of the flying feathered flock as a reprieve from all that sorority-house hullabaloo. One particularly bountiful November afternoon, he returned from the old homestead with a smorgasbord of birds for Ella to pluck.

And an eighty-pound Chesapeake Bay retriever. Bingo, which was henceforth his name, was rough and ready and raring to go. He was born to be a five-star pheasant fetcher and was a most welcome sidekick for Ed.

Unfortunately, Ella had decidedly different ideas about inviting that roustabout into her prim and proper parlor (picture doilies and doodads). She would not have the dog trampling her prized peonies, not wrinkling her well-starched world (we're talking ironed underwear). Since Viking wives do not harangue in public, it is assumed by all storytellers that there were spirited, closed-door discussions between Ella and Ed over the fate of poor Bingo. A stalemate ensued. Only, Bingo did himself no favors. The argument was firmly resolved with finality when Ella discovered her Sunday roast, last seen atop a snout-high stove, was being gulped down passionately—if not prudently—by the very defendant. She put her size 4 foot down. And so Bingo bought himself a return ticket to the boondocks.

Sometime later, Ella and Ed and the girls paid a call on their country cousins, where they were reunited with Bingo—tied up, forgotten, and despondent in his barnyard banishment. The sickening sight no doubt broke Ed's heart, but remarkably, it was Ella who reacted with righteous indignation at Bingo's situation. Though she may have had *Better Homes & Gardens* pride, it would not run roughshod over her moral compass. Immediately, they reclaimed Bingo, who then sprawled ecstatically among his favorite family for that snug car ride back to the city. Bingo, it seemed, had learned his lesson and was determined to earn his keep. He excelled as the crackerjack birder Ed had first discovered, both in the retrieval of grounded game and the retrieval of four lazy chicks asleep in the beds upstairs. Ed used Bingo for the former, Ella for the latter. She would send her trusty scout flying up the stairs to fetch the girls, and he wouldn't return until every last (not early bird) was rustled up. If it resulted in a bedsheet tug-o'-war, so be it. Bingo was bound to herd his human flock downstairs for breakfast at all costs.

It was as if Bingo understood the importance of his second chance. He ensured he endeared himself with newfound gentility. No more would he embark on mayhem among the blue-ribbon roses. If it would seem ironic that the one most opposed to Bingo would become his staunchest ally, it was anything but. For *of course* it was a given that any heart would soften at the pure, loveable hands—er, paws—of a pet like Bingo. It came as no surprise to anyone that Ella would step up to vigorously defend Bingo's indiscretions, including a particularly brisk once-over of a pip-squeak poodle down the block.

Bingo also made himself an equal-opportunity fan favorite when he would submit to all manner of high-style hats, hosiery, and ruby-red rouging at the hands of four budding glamour girls. Bingo was there through it all. As the girls grew up, left home, married, and had babies of their own, Bingo was still there until his last dog days.

There was an image on which the stories often ended: Ella, my tiny grandmother, devotedly hoisting that huge old boy, now too crippled to navigate those few small steps off the porch. Bingo died on the day of the last daughter's nuptials, as if he'd known he would be alone as the last of the four chicks flew from the nest. It was, to say the least, a weepy wedding party with a red-eyed bride.

There was, after that, a sorrowful stillness to house.

Traveling Nanny

I first met Minna Marie Chunda Chang Pauly, my new adopted baby niece, halfway around the world, somewhere near her humble place of birth. This was a pretty unlikely liaison, Minna and me, as babies are way out of my league. They are objects of aversion until deemed unbreakable, and I often did my best to bypass all but the most cursory perusals and requisite puffery over others' newborns.

Imagine everyone's surprise—including my own—when I impulsively volunteered to join my sister-in-law, Kristin, as her traveling nanny while she went to China to pick up her newly adopted daughter.

Decades earlier, as a young college student, Kristin gave birth to a baby, the product of a college flame. But the momentous weight of motherhood at that time was beyond Kristin's dorm-room dreams, so she chose to give the baby up for adoption. Twenty-one years later, Kristin met her son (a dead ringer for his biological uncle Chips). He was gracious as he squeezed his long-lost lineage onto a full family platter, but the bald truth was that he was someone else's son. Kristin knew it had been the right call to forfeit his wonder years to other hearts and hands, but a yearning for all those lost memories grew in Kristin's mind. Yet she was unattached and over the age of fifty. Could she really think of becoming a mother? The answer, as the rusted maternal floodgates were flung wide open, was a resounding yes.

While touched by the warmth and heart of Kristin's decision to adopt, I must admit I was unprepared to be emotionally engulfed as well. But when Minna was placed in her insta-mommy's arms, how could I not be moved? They were an unforgettable picture of perfect bliss.

Minna, a newborn female, had suffered the fate of so many unwanted baby girls in China. She'd been deposited at a railway station, then relegated to a bursting-at-the-seams orphanage for the first six months of her life, idling away in a pint-sized prison cell, warehoused among sardine rows of excess feminine. It baffled, astounded, and enraged me that a day-old daughter could be abandoned for want of a Y chromosome, but Minna was one of the fortunate few salvaged from that pitiful purgatory.

Minna, though, grew up in a home environment that was warm and fuzzy, and her heart seemed free of any festering angst about her tangled biological roots. She grew into a beautiful, sweet, stoic young woman with an old soul.

And to my delight, she also grew into a desire to collect furry friends—as many as Mom could be bamboozled into. And for every living pet Minna could convince her mom to keep, she had dozens of the stuffed-species variety to fill out Minna's Ark. At last count Minna's zoo boasted of four meowing members: wide-angled Waldo, who had lost his tail through some sketchy outdoorsman intrigue; loose-bladdered Lulu, a vaporous pee-and-flee pixie; and two redheaded shelter sisters, Honey and Sweetie, brokered under some sly two-for-one pretext by the wily Minna. She also had a yapping rag-mop of a dog, Zoie—a smooth tactical trade in lieu of a human little sister.

My own excessive animal emporium leads many (probably most) to believe that the cats and dogs are filling in for the biological little beasts I never bore. I'm not much for Freudian mind-sifting, but there might just be something to all that freshman-psych stuff. Like Minna, I, too, missed those earliest hugs and kisses, as I had remained in the hospital for the first month of my life. I wondered if our likeminded hairy hoarding habits covered some small psychic bare patch. No matter. Even if hosting a houseful of pets is some sort of emotional mortar, bighearted Minna would always love them.

Domestic Quarrels

In their bewitching babyhood, puppies and kittens are the easiest sell in the world. They are the odds-on favorites in the spare-pet roulette. But those scrumptious pip-squeaks inevitably turn into teenaged Tasmanian devils who dig, claw, climb, bite, and break their way toward sedate adulthood. The lowest among us throw in the towel at first blush of those inescapable growing pains, blaming the gangly troublemaker that took over that fuzzy toy they'd adopted instead of facing their own shortsighted ineptitude. (News flash, all you easy-come, easy-go pet pantywaists: Bic pens and Pampers are disposable, Fido and Fluffy are not.)

It doesn't help that people (wrongly) believe that they must have a dog from its puppy days to cement BFF status. But a long survey of our pet history upends that dangerous myth. It turned out that our not-puppy rescues became the biggest mama's boys and all-purr daddy's girls. I don't know if it's because of the dogs'—and cats'—gratitude for an easy life, or their nagging insecurities from a paw-to-mouth youth, or whether they're just making up for lost lap time, but whatever the superglue may be, our well-seasoned streetwalkers turned housecats and dogs are always the first on and last off any available lap. Even my longest-tooth rescues were steeped in the savoir faire of best-friends-for-hire.

But a word of warning. Talk to your spouse before jumping on the old-mutt bandwagon.

Chips would often joke that he'd have to write an autobiographic owner's manual titled *When Control Freaks Marry*. And yes, okay, so our consensus-building waltz could be a wee bit testy at times, a vigorous tug-of-war between a well-matched pair of verbal Vikings. I assure you, it was no small task to keep up with my silver-tongued sweetheart who got paid handsomely for his ability to navigate fine-print-infested conference calls and contractual quicksand without breaking a sweat. Somehow, with years of peppery practice and a vivid vocabulary, I was able to hold my own against Mr. Wonderful's word wizardry.

Case in point: the brief tenure of one rumpled old mutt that ignited a particularly memorable marital dustup between Super-Loophole Man and his fully clawed Cat Woman.

To set the scene, you must know of the emotional fortitude required to spend more than ten seconds at a pet-rescue center. It takes the toughness of an elephant's hide to deal with the endless ugly—and heartbreaking—reminders of human fallibility at its worst. How many second chances can there be? How can every dog or cat get theirs? The math is tragically lopsided, when you consider the number of souls up for adoption versus the number of souls with the power to adopt. The only way forward is to hoist up your big-girl britches, hone in on one lost little life at a time, and help mute the chaos with a small moment of love.

I was prepared. After beaucoup speed dates with every four-footed make and model at the pet-rescue Grand Central Station, I was far beyond any inadvertent take-home temptation. I was Teflon and tabby-proof. Not even the coyest crybaby could beckon me through the crossbars. I knew the rule, the bedrock of rescue centers everywhere: absolutely *no* favorites. Instead, I had to keep a firm grip on the big picture, or I'd be lost in that whirlpool of me-and-you-against-the-world in which I would elevate one love-starved pup over the droves of equally deserving others. Besides, our already stunningly high tail count of prowling Paulys was a constant, sobering reminder of the limits of time, space, and . . . well, yes, spousal support. So I gritted myself for the ear-piercing riot scene as every pup voiced a vigorous opinion to my passing by.

Except for one.

One mute mutt gave me curious pause. She was a rag mop, some hazy formulation of poodle, and genteel in a friendly, unassuming way, proper without a hint of self-import and immaculate decorum among the whacked-out alpha wannabes. She was no spring chicken; she was well into her double digits. Given the inverse ratio between age and adoption, her lack of BFF status was predictable; she would easily be beaten out by all those fuzzy freshman all-stars around her.

Call it Cupid (or just plain stupid), but those sweet eyes looked up at me and *bam!* All my love-'em-and-leave-'em bravado melted to the floor. I drove away with that incandescently happy dog—ignorant, unaware, and utterly delusional to the civil war awaiting me at home. In my mind, there would be no need for any argument. What was one more among our already eye-popping entourage? After all, as head zookeeper, I could divert a couple of more dollars to the herd-management debit column, and it would hardly register on Chips's penny-hugging radar. And surely our very own Daisy Mae, a renowned dog-despiser, would no doubt welcome my new, meek little tail-wagging friend. It seemed so simple. Put out another chow bowl and chew toy, and chalk one up for one more senior Cinderella.

And yet, my shining moment of white-knighthood seemed not to come with a matching suit of argument-proof armor. Instead, I was met with a red-hot husband who doused me into an ice-cold bath of reality. It stung all the more because I honestly didn't see it coming. I couldn't say who was the more shocked—Chips, for his astonished outrage over yet another needy deadbeat plunked down in his domain without so much as a spousal smoke signal, or me, for my baffled astonishment at all the blowback to such a benign little pip-squeak, or perhaps Daisy Mae for her dumbfounded disbelief at this affront to her exclusive Fido Fiefdom. Only my new Golden Girl kept her happy cool, despite all the growing, snarling, and snapping (and Daisy Mae made some pretty nasty noises, too).

Time didn't much mend our first-class domestic blowout, but we mutely called a truce and removed ourselves to our respective corners. To cover for my new girl's chilly welcome, I doubled up on the daily rations of love for the (now) lone ray of household sunshine. She was oblivious to Daisy's disgruntled evil eye and snide sneers and instead humbly happy to take her place at the bottom of the ranks.

And so we lived in a quiet truce. There was nothing to be done; even Chips conceded I was not going to return her to her previous fate. Then, one autumn day not long after, I found my poor girl, my unwitting troublemaker, belly-up, struggling in vain to plant her paws as Daisy Mae, her now-suddenly-sentimental mentor, prodded her to get up. I scooped up my panic-stricken girl and my heart sank at the sight of strange sludge seeping from her limp form. I raced my fallen angel to the vet. Tear-filled hours later, I returned home alone.

Now just in case you mistake my story for a cautionary tale, a painful lesson in responsible spousal communication, it wasn't. I was never one for regrets (Vikings do not have peepholes in the backs of their helmets), and I've never felt a pang of remorse for rewriting that old dog's short-but-sweet last chapter. Nor do I regret any other fur-coated impulses

I've succumbed to along the way. I concede that conversation is good—Chips deserved that at the very least—but to think I could turn away from a rescue opportunity? No. If I were to harbor regrets, it would only be that I wish I could have done, should have done more.

I was bitter for a long time after my parents' divorce. Sarcasm and me became great friends—enough that my actual friends would set up interventions. If I had longed for the type of optimism and hope Betsy wrote into her stories, the wish had been buried deep under layers of pain.

Yet, I realized, never once had I questioned the happily ever afters of romance. My own early dating history was a bust, yes, but when, after university, I met my future husband, I knew without a doubt he was the one. Though my parents had seemed happy to my oblivious child's eyes, and though the demise of their marriage and my family had turned me brittle, not once did I doubt the possibilities of a long-lasting, fulfilling marriage.

It turned out that, even then, in my darkest moments of trying to adjust to a new reality, there had always been a spark of hope. Optimism. Good humor. Laughter. Exasperation. Love.

By the time I read Betsy's stories, my character growth had already happened. Her stories didn't invoke a sudden, shocking aha moment into my life, but they did allow me to reflect on the growth I *had* made. It is easy, in the day-to-day grind of, well, living, especially as a mom, to lose perspective of how far one has come. Betsy's warmhearted tales of her family gave me the opportunity to do just that.

Chapter 16

When *Wonder Woman*, starring Gal Gadot, came out in 2017, there was a plethora of deserved praise for the movie. I, too, loved the action flick, but I was incensed by all the feminist hoopla surrounding it. By that I mean, I *supported* a feminist interpretation of the movie, and applauded Gadot's portrayal of Diana as strong and empathetic, a most welcome addition to the superhero canon, but I was also exasperated by the rhetoric. Yes, Diana was fierce and skilled. Yes, she took charge and saved the day. Yes, women could be all those things. Yes, they *are* all those things. But those are also typically *male* characteristics. Of *course* they shouldn't be—millions of women around the world have proven otherwise, but nonetheless, our western patriarchal society still holds those conventions to be true. So the *only* way for Diana to be hailed a feminist superhero was if she excelled at *male* tasks, duties, and skills? We could admire her only because she could compete with a traditionally male superhero?

I don't mean to disparage the character—I love Diana and I want to see more women like her on-screen—but you know what else I'd love to see? A superhero who happens to be female and excelling at traditionally *female* tasks, duties, and skills. I want to see the world celebrate a woman for saving the world through her knitting and her cooking, for her childcare and her domestic time management. I want to see society put *those* skills on a pedestal and venerate the incalculable contributions of the traditionally female role in the same high regard we honor shooting, killing, and fighting. Now *that* would be a true feminist superhero.

Instead, we must settle for venerating and celebrating the quiet superheroes among us, both male and female, whose superpower is care and empathy and helping others. Betsy, I have been arguing, is one of those. Betsy herself, no doubt, would deny such a label, and fair enough; she would be entitled to her opinion. But she was not above singling out her own superheroes in her life, most especially the vets who carried out her save-the-world-of-stray-animals mission with her.

Dr. Dolittles

A noble lineage of real-life Dr. Dolittles (a major misnomer for such industrious Do-a-Lots) have patched up our furry refugees through the years. Those busloads of broken-down lowlifes we've deposited for The Works would always return to us primed for carefree pethood from snout to stern, all at bargain-basement prices (imagine the astronomical balance due for your own such cavities-to-ovaries overhaul). Their white-coat curriculum is reputedly every bit as grueling as the infamous rigors of a doctor for humans. But upon graduation, Joe-Average DVM (more likely Josephine these days) deals with a clientele that doesn't talk in the local tongue (can't even point to the problems) or possess gainful employment with which to pay their bills, exhibit uncouth personal habits in the best of times (outright disgusting decorum at the first hint of exam-table trouble), and are at the mercy of careless, clueless, and otherwise fallible (and decidedly less lovable) humans. Despite the paw-panic certainty of clawing, biting, and back straining from disgruntled dogs and contortionist cats, and a howling inferno of chronic chaos around every flea-infested corner, it is, in fact, harder to gain entry to vet school than human medical school. I'm grateful for those big hearts and fearless hands, healing all hairy things great and small and, at the end, grieving with us in our great loss.

Along with our human superheroes in a vet's office, we'll often find spare cats whom the humans in charge have allowed free rein. They are often nosy little nomads, working the crowds in a wet-nosed waiting room. Often, they are natural-born busybodies and droll clowns, happy to entertain customers and their furry traveling companions with shelf-to-shelf acrobatics and cheeky lap liberties. Occasionally more timid cat mascots remain content to spy on the day's commerce perched on high. Understandably (in a fur-magnet manner I'm all too familiar with), the vets collect those loose-ended strays—unclaimed accounts receivable, semi-Samaritan drop-offs, or cats fired for any half-baked/hairbrained bailout baloney. No doubt, these angels of mercy try to put up a fur-proof firewall against falling for every cat, but while they are haloed, they are also human. And so one more cat appears in the office. But then, in my biased opinion, there really are far worse occupational hazards than bankrolling a few more love-starved kitties and pups along the way.

One such creature lived in Dr. Melanie's bustling clinic. Dr. Melanie was one of Mayberry's finest, with the beautiful ability to soothe my savage beasts with her delicate ministrations. When I came in one day in pursuit of my usual embarrassing tonnage of tabby groceries, I suddenly came toe-to-snarling-snout with eight cupcake-cute pounds of junkyard dog. Though he was adorable, he was also an ankle-high demon. I tried to bluff my way past his yippy *who's-the-alpha* chitchat, but my cheerful bravado and squeaky talk was met only with bared teeth—and the seemingly sincere promise to use them upon my person. I heeded the warning. While I gingerly detoured toward the industrial-sized chow bags, his red-faced employer rounded up her new sentinel (who had turned to silly putty in the boss's arms). Bandit (aptly named) had just been hired on as junior receptionist, rescued from a subpar situation before now. It explained his little bodyguard challenge to my hundred-and-plenty-pound self. Despite my welcome, however, I was thrilled for Bandit. He had landed in the best fur-caring hands that promised him a rosy future (though he had a daunting learning curve in diplomacy ahead of him).

Every return trip to Bandit's workplace/war zone meant another go-round with the dainty Tasmanian-devil doorman. He would still argue about some Crazy-Cat-Lady evildoing, but over time, his vitriol dwindled, diluted, as it were, with growing confidence. Slowly, he and I rewrote our regrettable beginning, and soon he would greet Dr. Melanie's customers with a happy yip and a welcoming wag. It would be so easy—and so wrong—to write off all the broken-down Bandits out there as lunatic lost causes, but thank God for all the miracle-working Dr. Melanies of the world and their unwavering faith in furry second chances.

I cannot sugarcoat our own angst, however. All of us who welcome in major fixer-uppers, from vets like Dr. Melanie to people like me, can inevitably slip into emotional quicksand despite our good intentions. We love the beasts for their noble longing, even if they end up disappointing.

Ziggy Quinn was one such sad mental case. He would bounce from best friend to deranged beast in an instant. He arrived with a mysterious grab bag of shortcomings, courtesy, no doubt, of not-so-wonderful Wonder Years. He showed the world a toothy grin and a windshield-wiper tail, but it covered nerves of Jell-O. A sneeze, for example, would elicit either dog-in-the-headlights paralysis (stalling out along his walk and making it extraordinarily difficult to budge his eighty-pound shellshocked body), or he would bark in a don't-mess-with-me-or-I'll-tear-you-limb-from-limb fashion. His discombobulated radar was always ricocheting between those fight-or-flight flip-sides, and as such, he would often cling to me (who, really, wasn't much bigger than him). Or he would barricade me against evil interlopers, including, but not limited to, an overstuffed armchair to which he'd taken a distinct dislike. One would have to brace against his gates-of-hell greeting—his gauntlet thrown down, with only the bravest alpha guests willing to pick up. But then, *poof!* The growling gangster would be gone, and his shaggy alter-boy alter ego would reappear with the most convincing *pet-me-please* whimper.

He was a handful.

And he was a good reminder that I *did* understand the frustrations and lamentations of pet ownership. I wearied in my care of Ziggy Quinn. I wished for a magic wand to keep him at his friendliest best, but alas, I never found one. Instead, I did what was hard—and heartbreaking—to do. I just kept going.

Isn't that the best we can do?

The Eden Alternative

I always found it shortsighted that we limit our animal time to the day's few after-work hours. Wouldn't we most benefit from those purveyors of positivity when we need them most—at our hair-pulling primetime? Is it not a sad commentary on our topsy-turvy priorities? Shouldn't the widest wedge of who we are be reserved for those who are most important to us? I understand not all cats and dogs can join all us humans in the workplace, but wouldn't it be wonderful if they could? Wouldn't Fido or Fluffy dispel the drudgery that threatens to zombie-trudge us right out the door?

Any boss worth her salt would appreciate the trickle-up economics of a happy staff fueled with puppy love. Cats and dogs in the workplace would transcend office politics and prime our creative pumps. Wouldn't that be worth it?

My brother Jon, a doctor, thought so. He invited a parade of pint-sized, furry-coated "social workers" to join him and his staff in nurturing seniors. Jon's silk-and-swanky standards put the traditional sit-and-rot seniors' homes to shame. The revolutionary Eden Alternative (the new how-to-grow-old gold standard) commuted the waiting-for-death aura of other over-eighty residences into places drenched with life. Their strategy was simple: We all need something to do, someone to admire, and a sweet place to call home. Think about the little things that light our dark corners—a four-year-old's finger painting, music to match our Brahms-to-Beatles mood, tulips at breakfast, or a ball of purring fur at your fingertips. It is life's perfectly imperfect minutiae, the everyday details, that remind us who we are and where we belong.

Argyle was the embodiment of this very notion. Every morning, the vigilant cat would take first watch atop his ledge of medical files, on the lookout for Jon and his daily head scratch. He was, in fact, the head of a crew of ex-alley allies, a mixed bag of pound hounds and a campus of feathered and finned friends working the seniors crowd. Argyle and his brethren were the extra-strength Rx necessary to simmer down blood pressures (dose: one dog, taken daily, enough to offer up a paw-powered endorphin). Even the lowliest of mutt comes fully equipped to blast the blue-funk away. If you've ever had a dog walk your worries away, or felt a lap purr melt away a bad day, you already know that kind of magic. A stroll through Argyle's world summed up all the science nicely—those natural-born miracle workers dispel brain fog and frowns; they offer up their very own brand of medicine to all takers in a bark-filled ark of geriatric joy.

Is it any wonder why I see Betsy as a quiet, determined superhero in her own right?

Chapter 17

In our late twenties, Scott and I had the opportunity to live in Tanzania for a summer while I taught English in a small rural village. We already owned a house and two cats, so obviously, we had to make arrangements. The house was easy; our families were happy to check on it during our absence. The cats were hard. Everyone we knew either had pets already (and those pets most definitely did *not* share their owners), had allergies, or had no capacity to take care of our two little beasts—each weighing more than twenty pounds, no matter how long they were on diet cat food!

Except for our friend Rachel.

Only, she lived on the other side of the country.

So what did we do? Only the best for our cats . . . we flew them from Ottawa to their summer home in Halifax. (Later, I would fly the same route with two very young children and had by then learned to appreciate how little a parent could control the cries, sounds, and discomfort of another living thing. I think that first flight with our two cats had prepared me.) Simon and Sebastian, snug in individual cat carriers, fit beneath the seats in front of us. They each meowed pitifully, to my great embarrassment, but, to my great reprieve, not loudly. Still, I was on edge the entire flight.

It was only an hour and a half.

Except for the flight home at the end of that summer, I have never again traveled with animals. No great calamity befell us; there was no nightmare scenario, no horror of misadventure—just low-level angst I had no interest in repeating. On planes, trains, or automobiles.

So when I read Betsy's story entitled "Road Trip," I was flabbergasted. I reread it. And read it again. Then I asked Chips, "Wait, you traveled where? With how many cats and dogs? And how many times a year? For how many years??"

He just laughed.

Road Trip

One year, we found ourselves in possession of Chips's childhood home in Minnesota and, as such, we found ourselves contemplating an annual migration for the state's trio of vaguely temperate months (truthfully, about three warmish weeks surrounded by weather only tough-as-nails Norsemen would call nice). With ease, we ripped down all the logistical roadblocks to our plan—save one glaring obstacle. Our menagerie. Leaving our gang of loveable good-for-nothings behind for those summer journeys was a drop-dead dealbreaker. Yet were we really prepared to transport our herd in a dawn-to-dusk drive-a-thon?

Yes, yes we were.

But cats are unapologetic homebodies. A solid web anchors the consummate control freaks to their fiefdom; any loose threads end up tangled like two-sided tape in the wind. Whether frantically pawing at the blank space of a beloved potted plant suddenly gone AWOL, quizzically surveying wandering wingback chairs (one should never relocate a royal throne), or raising hackles over some menacing new throw pillow, cats are attuned to everything. Household minutiae never flies under that hypervigilant radar.

Consequently, as all survivors of such hellish misadventures are painfully aware, traveling with Team Tabby is a profoundly unnatural event. There are vague rumors of car-happy kitties, dreamily dozing on dashboards, peacefully perusing the passing world. That was not our own bountiful pet destiny. Even the most zen of our cats went ballistic when his built-in gyroscope started spinning out of kitty kilter. When you consider that even the briefest sprint to that notorious house of horror, or, as we humans call it, the vet, can incite inconsolable anguish, a long drive is, to them, inconceivable.

Yet we planned to uproot our fragile hothouse flowers for the dreaded road trip. Mallards and monarchs, whales and wildebeest, Laplanders and Learjet-ers all get that *let's-go* urge. Cats do not. Regardless, we remained firm in our plans for our woeful band of oddballs and misfits—already skating on wafer-thin emotional ice at the best of times.

Obviously, if they'd had voting privileges, our little hermits would have selected uninterrupted residence in their current habitat, but I preferred not to languish in illusions. Therefore, (a) as cats do not have any obvious hopes and dreams beyond momentary pleasure-seeking, nor a sufficient command of English to enunciate any such wishes, and (b) as cats do not savor variety as the truest spice of life, sleeping away the bulk of their existence, and (c) as cats do not emote one iota of altruism concerning the wants and needs of others (always *me*-ow, *me*-ow), and (d) as cats do not pay the bills, and (e) as cats do not possess sufficient paw power for wheel-turning, brake-tapping, and passing out salty snacks and Snapple, the aimless furry freeloaders are dictatorially relegated to where we say. In this case, the back seat.

It was a vast universe-gaping chasm between the cats' attitude and our dog's. Though Daisy Mae had died by the time we started our cross-country adventures, she would have shone with unbridled enthusiasm. There would have been no need for a Purina-punctured please to get her in the car. Where we were treated with accusing glares by our churlish Chat Noir entourage, we would have gotten only loving looks from our pup. If anything, her omnipresence would have been somewhat pesky as we tried to prepare. When the car door opened, for example, our road warrior would have been doing a happy dance on the Louis Vuitton luggage. There wouldn't have been enough Beggin' Strips on the planet to bribe Daisy Mae back out of the vehicle. Facing forward, ready for anything, she had always been calm in the confidence that she'd never be left behind. There'd never been a happier being.

And so we set out, hauling our herd north and south across the Mason-Dixon Line, back and forth, back and forth. It was just one ear-nose-and-throat-numbing day, door-to-door, quite the hike, but certainly manageable in our school bus of a Suburban.

It took some finesse, I grant you, as we bought then stacked cages that ate up every last unoccupied inch of our Suburban. As the straggling Easter snow gave way to spring, we set up our gypsy van, then corralled a *very* reluctant bunch of animals into assigned seating. From dumbfounded disbelief to manic prison-break bombardments, each sad little face looked to us for an explanation of this moving madness. I actually couldn't blame them. When I would collapse into the driver's seat, already two pit stops and a bag of Cheetos behind schedule and nearing my wit's end, I could only ask myself the same reproachful questions. *What in the heck were we thinking?* Why had we thought it was a good idea to uproot our neurotic herd of homebodies for a few months, only to turn around and repeat that twelve-hour torture chamber—uh, drive—once again?

And through it all, Chips remained my coolheaded copilot. My unflappable Mr. Fix-It held his steely focus as he talked me through my meltdown.

Finally creeping out of the driveway after checking the last of the checklist, and taking a few deep yoga breaths, I felt my roll-with-the-karmic-punches spirits returning. The animals, too, ran out of steam. All was now peace, love, and understanding behind me, nary a pip-squeak peep. My faith in our routines-are-for-chumps road-warrior life had been renewed.

Oh, but then we decided to make life complicated.

We bought a house in Florida.

And drove our menagerie there and back, too.

This epic eight-state marathon called for a lot more leg room for our thirteen cats. Our Suburban wasn't going to cut it, so we came up with a beautiful solution to our critter-commuting conundrum: a travel trailer.

We'd already frittered away weeks of Saturdays drifting through those RV shows in a *someday* fog, dreaming up footloose fifth-wheeling and slo-mo motor-coach meanderings, yet always we walked away empty-handed. However, we now had rock-solid justification with our impending interstate loop the loop. Like two middle-aged kids in a candy store, we drooled over every pop-up, pullout, and Winnebago wannabe Chips could wrestle between the white lines. (I admit I set aside my well-worn chauffeur's cap and chickened out of piloting any such lane-swaying, jackknifing, big-as-barn rig.) Finally, we fell hard for that dangerously cool Johnny-Depp-of-rolling-real-estate, the Airstream. Though Chips may have watched our pennies over the small stuff, when it came to thinking (and spending) big, my sweetheart took the budget-busting cake (buying houses in a matter of minutes, driving a countless number of cars off the lot on a lark, and falling in love at first sight with mobile residences like the trailer).

And can you believe it? Those darn cats went on to prove their patently selfish nature. Although we procured the trailer almost exclusively for their comfort, Sunny, Bunny, Peter Pan, Snowman, Mr. Mitt, Festivus, Atticus, Tinkerbell, Baby Lily, Gretel, Chippy, Jimmy, and Ginger *all* unanimously rejected our magnificent gypsy wagon outright, insisting they'd rather stay put.

But we'd learned long ago how fruitless a request for cooperation among that bunch of anarchists was, so we didn't ask for a show of paws before escorting our Dirty Baker's Dozen into their deluxe conscript cabin. Each cat got a princess-and-the-pea-padded private sleeping berth, copious Tidy Cat commodes (in case a couple were *ocupado* all day by spineless squatters), and plenty of captive colleagues to commiserate over such shabby treatment. Needless to say, containing that riot of freaked-out felines was no small feat (and a half a happy pill didn't take all the *what-the-hell?!* wind out of their scrappy little sails). With our shell-shocked prisoners trying to bolt at every crack of the jailhouse door, Chips and I developed impressive four-armed choreography. And somehow we kept all the crazed cats corralled, with every last lunatic passenger finally secured in assigned seating.

The free (with $50,000 purchase) Airstream calendar we got was full of charming vignettes promising carefree adventure around every beautiful bend. I have to say, it didn't quite do justice to the dizzying array of hair-raising incidents during our maiden voyage. We hadn't even torn open the first bag of Cheetos when a flat tire was kindly brought to our addled attention by a passing motorist. *That* most certainly deflated that initial surge of giddy wanderlust. Instead, we were reduced to silent prayers to the patron saint of discombobulated travelers.

It got worse.

In search of a new tire, we got stranded on a theoretically closed exit ramp courtesy of my nerve-racked, below-average navigator talents (further clouded by a blinding desire to call it a day), where we met up with a heartily amused road crew doubled over in hysteria at our efforts to avoid becoming one with the freshly tarred surface we crept over. (Note to all prospective twenty-five-foot-trailer pullers: Attempting U-turns on a one-way, single-lane, elevated ramp is ill-advised.)

Finally, in the black of night, we made it to our very-shabby-but-not-so-chic campsite, well within earshot of a neighboring highway's Indy 500 roar (and far removed from our RV directory's claim of pastoral peace). It was the last straw that tipped my not-so-happy-camper scale over the edge on that memorable first day of nomadic life. My Rock-of-Gibraltar hubby (always a Cool-Hand-Luke customer, crises being his legal bread and butter) somehow worked some wife-whisperer magic on my flat-as-a-pancake spirit, quietly convincing me that giving up—and conceding to a sixty-square-mile sedentary existence forevermore—was not the answer. Only then, as I lay, wide-eyed and waiting for sleep, could I finally smile at the day's dark comedy.

The remainder of that teeth-gritting trip overflowed with more trials and terrors: a soda-spilling, bottom-busting, brain-bending jaunt along the entire potholed length of Arkansas; a Mario Andretti obstacle course of ricochet lane changes and cryptic turnoffs in Memphis (sorely tempted as we were to take the Graceland exit and pay our respects to the King, neither of us held much hope of backtracking through that tangled old city with two thousand pounds of tin and one hundred pounds of hairball); the play-by-play of an all-night tractor pull within Skoal-spittin' distance in Mississippi; and bobbing and weaving along with a sea of bumper-to-bumper early birds through the thunderously waterlogged Sunshine State. Finally, weary Captain Chips parked for good, while his bedraggled copilot kissed the ground beneath her wobbly feet, the blessed end of that long and winding road.

There are people in this world who cannot take responsibility for their actions; they blame others, the environment, society, and the world. To be fair, others, the environment, society, and the world *can* cause distress, debacles, calamities, and *cat*astrophes, but so, too, can our own whims and desires. Understanding when to accept our own hand in our fate—and then laugh about it—is a rare skill. Betsy, clearly, excelled.

So it was not that Betsy was determined to travel cross-country with her furry menagerie that made her a crazy cat lady; it was that she could, no matter the hair-pulling challenges, poke gentle fun at herself for her choices. I mean, really, what type of person drives thirteen cats back and forth across the U.S.?

Maybe the same type who would fly her cats back and forth across Canada.

Chapter 18

Sebastian was my favorite cat. Am I allowed to say that? Can we secretly like one cat or one dog among our storied history of pet ownership more than the others? Or are they meant to be like children, that we love them all equally, in their own right? Well, if cats could read, then perhaps I'd think twice about pouring my (unjust) heart out onto the page, but given that cats and dogs can have a favorite human, I am inclined to allow myself the same luxury.

It's not that I adored Sebastian's brother Simon any less. Nor do I hate any of our four very distinct current cats. I am a softie, it turns out, as unable to move a comfortable cat from the couch as much as anyone else in my household.

But Sebastian nudged himself into the deepest recesses of my heart by his damnable, incessant, ***adorable*** insistence that he get petting on command and a warm lap upon which to curl no matter our own human needs. Some might have found this behavior irksome at best, and might have been ready to dropkick the damned cat at worst, but for reasons I still have trouble analyzing, I found it endearing. Perhaps it was that I'd never had a pet as a child. Perhaps I loved the idea of proving all those dog people with superior attitudes wrong about the unconditional love for which a cat could show his people. Perhaps I just simply loved to cuddle up with the big fluffball. No matter the reason, Sebastian became my cuddle cat, and though I hoped for the same burrowing charm in the next four, I was out of luck. Ivy is much too skittish—the term *scaredy-cat* was invented to explain her. Holly simply likes to curl up on her own. Angel is a flophouse of a cat; put her anywhere and she's happy, but rarely does she seek out her people. And Shadow, oh dear lord, Shadow. She loves to climb on your lap. If you have a book, or a tablet, or anything that's getting in her way of your attention. And she will then climb into your face—literally. (I've had scratch marks to prove it.) She is the prima donna in our household, and, obviously, she knows it. If she wants attention, she won't cozily curl up with you; she will ***demand*** it with all her queenly powers.

When Simon was alive, he loved to be near but not on. He would prance after us from room to room, then settle on the ground near—not at—our feet. Close, but not too close. So, yes, it was only Sebastian who gave me all the cuddly love I loved. He died of old age; I couldn't regret his passing, though I mourned him.

But, like people, Sebastian was an original.

Still, I had to wonder. ***Am I cruel to harbor such emotions?*** It begs the question: ***Does anyone else feel the same as me?***

Oh thank God for Betsy.

Yes, yes, it turned out. For all Betsy's plethora of furry friends, she, too, had a soft spot for one particular cat.

She was like me.

Festivus Magnificus

I was the notorious neighborhood dog catcher, but Chips had rounded up plenty of free-range fur, too. Most infamously was Festivus Magnificus. And while the rest of Mr. Wonderful's catches had all moved on to good lives beyond our four walls, I confess I bore the burden for this single statistical blemish (a moot technicality—there was zero chance my resident voice of reason would relinquish his turned-up treasure).

Chips and Festivus Magnificus began their fabled friendship in the parking lot of Mayberry's miniature country club. He was walking inside when he spied the dirty dust mop of a cat and thus assured the persistent panhandler he'd inquire as to his ownership. An hour later, Chips reemerged; immediately the desperate little dumpster diver made another beeline directly for Chips. Flabbergasted, Chips watched, open-mouthed, as the little kitty charged ahead toward Chips's car and then hopped confidently into the passenger seat.

Shaking his head, Chips left with the cat. He'd had a plan to smuggle the rescue into our spare room, then at daybreak, he'd sneak him back out for a clandestine visit to a Dr. Dolittle. Chips rightly feared I would display unguarded infatuation for this down-and-out dreamboat and would thus erase any hope of my own professional matchmaker impartiality. In other words, one look at this cat, and I'd force Chips to let him stay.

Now, it is true that I was the alleged weak link in all things cat, though I forcefully contest the title. My big, burly he-man husband was as incapable of hurling a semibelievable "no" at a naughty-clawed cat as I was. But I admit that Chips's top-secret scheme to get the new rescue out of the house before I saw him was a good one.

Only, Chips forgot to factor in my early-bird bladder, and so I awoke to mysterious thumps and bumps overhead. Immediately my twenty questions drowned out Chips's back-pedaling explanations. And then I saw the new addition. The little cat gazed up at me, blinked a slow-motion kitty kiss, and put a velveteen vise grip on my heart.

Chips had been right to be worried.

Yet still, he resigned himself (none too painfully, I might add) to racking up one more rescue, elevating our herd to a breathtaking baker's dozen. Yes, yes, yes, I phoned in furry "Found" ads, and so what if I was tickled pink that there was no response? Of *course* we didn't need yet another little moocher, but among all the nervous Nellies and habitual hermits that no one else would touch with a ten-foot pet pole, this new rescue finally gave us a doorbell-ready mascot.

And so, Festivus Magnificus made us his home.

He would sit by the sink and shower in the mornings, gnawing on his very own toothbrush, then meander among a desk covered in contracts and cats before planting himself in Chips's ever-ready lap.

Fes was everything to us, including, I believed, a reincarnation of my father, deceptively downsized but hardly downgraded. Yes, it was strange to think of puss as Pop, but the parallels persisted. Right from the first instance Fes found his way into Chips's car—my *dad's* old car. And what about those interchangeable salt-and-pepper manes? The Buddha bellies? The un-Fluffy-ish culinary craving? Raspberries, olives, a Budweiser with a V8 chaser . . . though just a tiny taste of near-beer for the little one. Any last doubts about some spiritual hitchhiking have long since vanished. Forget logic and its laundry list of question marks. I just rejoiced in that close-knit karma. Only, I was left wondering about all the other recycled souls among us.

Chapter 19

Here are Betsy's last words on the subject of cats.

Note her use of the present tense.

Note her optimism for a future that, yes, is our past.

But still today, and into our own future, Betsy's message rings true.

See Change

Honestly, I didn't start out this way. I hadn't given stray cats and alley cats and rescue cats anything more than a passing sigh. Until one whiskery kindness mushroomed into another and then another, and then a dozen more, and more again. Suddenly, I found myself (poorer and) in a new quasi-career as a psycho-puss therapist. And a new moral crusade to stop litterbugs—of the disposing-of-cats variety. Yes, I grant you that my Costco-size inventory of living leftovers looks a little (well, maybe a lot) like a furry episode of *Hoarders*, and that a casual observer might shake one's head before or after shouting, "Nutcase!" Believe it or not, I actually think one cat or two would be ideal. I didn't set out to save the kitty world; I'm not sure I even *wanted* the job, to be frank. But what exactly was I supposed to do? Toss all those basket cases stuck under my bed back out onto the lean, mean streets?

Not gonna happen.

So I leaned into my destiny. I leaned into counting cats like I was an insomniac counting sheep. I leaned into constructing the most epic charts and checklists for even the most seasoned of critter sitters. I leaned into my spokescat role, doling out Fluffy-care dos and don'ts with TV-evangelist fervor. I admit I was a shameless spare-kitty huckster, a semihysterical haranguer for *hiss*terectomies, an overheated Maltese-mill harpoon, all for a captive audience—you know, like creeping Kroger lines, coach class on planes (for contortionists only), Christmas-card fodder, with precious little concern for polite niceties or perceived mental status. Now I wear my Crazy Cat Lady badge proudly. I have, I am confident, earned my card-carrying credential.

I'm also tickled pink to report, years after my crusade commenced, that there is rising groundswell of really good news. I don't know exactly when or where the incoming tidal wave of furry flotsam turned, but it has. The grassroots gumption of do-gooders has granted many overcrowded towns a reprieve from the steady stream of animals finding their way to the city pound—and to the "good-night" needle. Cheap-to-free spay/neuter programs and two-tiered dog tags are only a few of the ways we've managed to stem the tide of overbreeding.

I tip my hat to superhero pet stores that have played matchmaker. PetSmart alone has connected five million love-starved leftover mutts and kitties with critter-crazy customers. Yes, that's five million! (I get goosebumps every time I see all those zeros!) And it's pure PR genius, to boot. How best to increase sales? Increase customers! But I don't see crass; I see care. Who says nice guys finish last?

And, if we dig down on those stats, millions more second chances means millions fewer puppy-dungeon mills. The more we adopt, the more we curb demand.

In other words, it's cool to be kind, and the contagion is catching. Gold-plated pound puppies grabbing Super Bowl suds, Oscar nods (here, here, Uggie the furry actor!). And then there's the media's four-pawed propaganda, like *Animal Planet,* prying open rusty-hinged hearts and minds. Just try to hitch a ride with Detroit's finest on their gut-wrenching ghetto-pet patrol, or stay tuned for K9 prison pals warming the souls of their equally outcast incarcerated keepers with puppy love, without a full box of Kleenex.

There's so much forward momentum to cheer about, so many hard-won high fives for every second chance at a well-worn leash and a forever lap. I offer great big hugs to all my alley-tramping/nonstop-poop-scooping/forever-Fluffy-hustling heroes out there, everyday angels among us.

Because here's the bottom line: It's not nearly enough to turn all our do-gooding inward, worshipping only our own lucky little prince charming. Think about all the untitled others, skulking down alleys, sleeping under the neighbor's shed, languishing in last-chance limbo—missing that one simple thing, a home. Why not be their hero, too?

After I had read Betsy's full manuscript, I had asked myself, *What is it about her draft, her work, her stories that make me feel not just that I am reading about her experiences, not just that I am reading about* her, *but that I am* meeting *her? How has she made me feel, simply by reading her work, that I am* already *her friend?*

I learned of her sass, her humor, her generosity. I learned of her passion and her heart. I learned of her gentleness and ferocity. I learned of a Betsy who was a quiet hero to animals and friends alike but who was also far from perfect.

I learned there were traits of hers I admired. I learned there were some things we had in common and some things we did not.

Through her stories, though they were about her animals, I saw Betsy. I saw authenticity, and more, I saw how authenticity could connect us to others.

So yes, it made sense to me why I would be attracted to her spirit; but had I discovered how I could so adamantly claim *her* friendship?

Indeed, I had.

Ironically, my answer was in my very question.

Betsy had made me feel I was *already* her friend because that's the way Betsy made me *feel*.

It's not about what could have happened or would have happened in real life. Friendship isn't only what we do, nor how long we've known each other, nor how often we see each other. Friendship is, at heart, how we make each other *feel*. Loved, supported, trusted.

Seen.

Betsy showed me, through her stories, how she was her truest, most authentic self.

Betsy showed me, through her stories, we can connect with others *because* we are our most authentic selves.

Betsy therefore showed me, through her stories, how to *feel* like my own authentic self.

Betsy may not have known me personally, but she opened herself up on the page, inviting me—and all who read her stories—into her world.

And it is in that very invitation, in the very act of making me feel *seen* in my own authenticity, that Betsy and I became friends.

Epilogue

"Betsy developed a cough that she thought was an allergy," Chips recalled. "It didn't clear up. She said, 'Let's go to Missouri, where I'll get different air, and maybe my cough will clear up.' So we went to the house in Missouri, but it didn't. She had to sleep sitting up; she was coughing too bad if she lay down. Finally, she met with a doctor; later, he and the radiologist would show me her X-rays. Betsy's lungs, which were supposed to look dark gray, instead looked like they were covered in spiderwebs. 'We have no idea what this is,' they said. We had to call it cancer because it was invasive, but there was no tumor."

Chips explained they returned to Florida, did more blood tests, and found Betsy had a genetic marker that put her in a very small universe of people. But there was a new drug that could treat cancer in that universe of people. She took the medicine and got back to what appeared to be normal health. For a few years, the drugs helped. One doctor even said Betsy may never need chemo, suggesting she would outlive Chips.

She didn't.

One night, when Chips returned from a trip to Missouri, Betsy went into the hospital. The doctor didn't understand what was wrong. "She doesn't look sick," he said.

"Her lungs aren't working properly," Chips insisted.

The doctor considered. "Well, we'll open up her lungs, keep her overnight, and tomorrow you two can go home."

Chips paused before he finished the story.

"That's not what happened."

Chips shared one last story.

"One night when we were in Minneapolis we thought Festivus had eaten a ribbon. Betsy was worried for his health, so we headed to an all-night vet. It was midnight. There was one car in the parking lot, and one woman in the back with the vet. Her cat busted loose and started running around the lobby, trying to get away, he was so scared. The woman, distraught, raced out to nab her cat and bring him back to the examining room. Betsy and I looked at the vet tech behind the desk.

"'Her cat ate Tylenol,' he explained. 'His kidneys are shutting down. They're going to have to put him down.'

"In the meantime, the vet came out and treated Festivus, who it turned out had not eaten any ribbon, so we got to go home with a healthy cat. As we were leaving, we noted the condition of the woman's car in the parking lot. It was missing a hubcap, and the paint was messed up. This was obviously a woman of very limited means. Betsy and I got in our car. She stared out the window, not moving.

"'Go pay her bill,' she said. She didn't look at me.

"I went inside. 'I want to pay the bill for that lady,' I told the vet tech.

"'What are you talking about?'

"'It's sad enough she's going to have her cat killed; she shouldn't have to pay for it.'

"He started to cry, went in the back, and returned with the amount. I paid it.

"'You can never tell her who we are, or never give her our name,' I pleaded. 'Just tell her the bill is taken care of.'"

Chips again paused in his recollection. Then he smiled.

"That's who Betsy was."

Acknowledgments

It was an unusual experience, obviously, to write a memoir with a coauthor who is no longer with us, but I wasn't alone. Thanks to Chips Pauly, Betsy's husband, for not only help with the interviews, the logistics, and the nuts and bolts of this project but also for his beautiful dedication to his wonderful wife. Because Chips kept striving to honor Betsy through her stories, you, like me, got the opportunity to "meet" her.

Chips also wanted to offer his own gratitude, for which I am honored: "Thanks to Jen Braaksma who had both the insight to recognize Betsy was a special person and the skills to present Betsy's stories in an engaging manner."

It was, as you've read, my absolute pleasure to do so.

About the Authors

Jen Braaksma

photo: Annemarie Grudën

Jen Braaksma is the author of two young-adult novels, *Evangeline's Heaven* and *Amaranth*. A former journalist and high school English teacher, Jen is now a book coach, helping writers develop their stories. She lives in Ottawa, Canada, with her husband (soulmates do exist!), two daughters (Best. Kids. Ever.), and four cats (who *know* they're in charge).

Betsy Pauly

photo: Chips Pauly

Originally from Minneapolis, Betsy earned her degree in business before taking on the corporate world. She began painting professionally in 1986, then turned to writing in 2010. Over the years, Betsy rescued more than one hundred cats, at least ten dogs, and one blind pigeon. With her husband, Chips, she lived in Dallas, Texas; Carthage, Missouri; and Englewood, Florida before her death in 2016. For more information about Betsy's artwork and cats in this book, visit www.befriendingbetsy.com.

Looking for your next great read?

We can help!

Visit www.shewritespress.com/next-read
or scan the QR code below for a list
of our recommended titles.

She Writes Press is an award-winning
independent publishing company founded to
serve women writers everywhere.